OUR BEST
RECIPES FROM

GRANDMA'S
COOKIE JAR

To cooks everywhere who want to bake easy, fun and delicious cookies for their family & friends.

Gooseberry Patch
An imprint of Globe Pequot
64 S. Main Street
Essex, CT 06426

www.gooseberrypatch.com
1 800 854 6673

••••••••••••••••••••••

Do you have a tried & true recipe... tip, craft or memory that you'd like to see featured in a **Gooseberry Patch** cookbook? Visit our website at **www.gooseberrypatch.com** and follow the easy steps to submit your favorite family recipe.

Or send them to us at:
Gooseberry Patch
PO Box 812
Columbus, OH 43216-0812

Don't forget to include the number of servings your recipe makes, plus your name, address, phone number and email address. If we select your recipe, your name will appear right along with it... and you'll receive a FREE copy of the book!

CONTENTS

Cookies! Cookies!
Cookies!
4

:::::::::::::::::::::

Rolled & Shaped Cookies
8

**Easy Icebox &
No-Bake Cookies**
34

Brownies & Blondies
56

**Fancy & Specialty
Cookies**
86

**Favorite Drop
Cookies**
112

Cut-Out Cookies
154

Beautiful Bar Cookies
172

Holiday & Party Cookies
224

:::::::::::::::::::::

Index 248

Cookies! Cookies! Cookies!

We know them as a "just-a-bite" treat, a little morsel of sweetness or a "pick-me-up" goodie. Yum. The word "Cookies" makes us smile as we imagine all the possibilities. And the basic truth about cookies is this: Many start out with the simple dough ingredients of flour, sugar, butter and eggs. Other ingredients, such as rolled oats, chocolate or peanut butter, may be added for flavor and texture. Cookies come in all shapes and sizes and the method to make them can vary from no baking at all, to baking complex layers of cookie goodness. And one of the nicest aspects of cookie-making is that often it is about a multi-generational event, with great-grandmas and grandmas passing along their skills to moms and children. How sweet is that? Here are a few categories of cookies that will get you started on your cookie journey:

Rolled & Shaped Cookies

You don't need fancy cutters and utensils for rolled and shaped cookies. Nimble fingers will suffice. This cookie category carries names such as Molasses Sugar Cookies, Peanut Butter Kisses (with the chocolate star or candy kiss in the middle of the peanut butter cookies), Pecan Cookie Balls, Fudgy Cappuccino Crinkles and Snickerdoodles. Perhaps you want to make dough balls to roll in powdered sugar after baking. They just need a little bit of finishing before serving. The dough of rolled cookies is gathered into a ball, and put directly on the prepared pan, sometimes slightly pressed down with an upside-down jar lid or fork. Sometimes the dough can be shaped and rolled into various shapes such as ropes, before baking. Often the dough works best when it has been chilled to facilitate rolling.

Icebox Cookies & No-Bake Cookies

Two types of cookies, icebox or refrigerator cookies and no-bake

cookies, were a reflection of their times. From surviving the Depression through World War II, homemakers developed a need to prepare foods efficiently. They used simple ingredients at hand and a spoon and a bowl. Cookies known as Cocoa No-Bakes and Hopscotch Cookies call for chocolate or butterscotch chips, coconut and peanut butter for texture and flavor. To make them, cooks simply dropped teaspoonfuls of cookie mixture onto wax paper and let form into yummy cookies. Icebox or refrigerator cookies worked under the same premise. The dough was shaped in long rolls, about one to 3 inches in diameter, then chilled long enough to make it easy to slice. If desired, the dough could be layered and rolled up and then sliced for a simply stunning look. A guest drops in? Simply slice off some cookies and bake them. Serve warm cookies to the company. Easy-peasy.

Brownies & Blondies

Likely known as the nation's top bar cookie, brownies, frosted or unfrosted, take the cake. Blondies are the lighter-toned version. They were an early convenience dessert. Just bake in a rectangular or square pan, cut into squares, and serve. They can be enhanced with the addition of peanut butter, pecans, and various icings; plus, for serving, they can be cut in squares and diamond shapes. Or, for transporting to a friend's house or to a potluck gathering, they are easily carried in the pan in which they were baked. Brownies were introduced at the Chicago World's Fair in 1893. Immigrants to the United States who took cooking classes in Boston and Philadelphia learned to make the treats in their classes.

Fancy & Specialty Cookies

Sometimes events call for fancier cookies, such as Macaroons, Kringla, Crunchy Biscotti, Italian

Cheese Cookies or Window-Pane Cookies. As showy as they are, they are worth the extra time to create them. The recipe for French Macaroons calls for almond flour and is a sandwich-style cookie with chocolate ganache or buttercream icing. Norwegian Kringla recipes turn out figure 8-shaped cookies, lovely on a mixed cookie tray. Enjoy them glazed or buttered. All of these fancy and specialty cookies are fun to make and bring lots of "oohs and aahs" from the cookie lovers you serve them to.

Favorite Drop Cookies

Drop cookies are a lovely gift to make for those you love. They are simple, quick to make easily and full of love. What more could you ask? It's why the classic Chocolate Chip Cookie has hung on for so long. It fits in all the categories, and its classic taste is a favorite of most cookie-munchers. Other cookie recipes, too, fit into this category from Monster Cookies, Oatmeal Raisin and Peanut Butter Cookies to drop cookies filled with fruits and nuts. You just can't beat stirring up a batch of drop cookies to share within the hour!

Cut-Out Cookies

Cut-out cookies, often sugar or gingerbread cookies, help us celebrate such events as holidays, baby showers, anniversaries, corporate events and, yes, even weddings for those who don't prefer cake. Early on, when cookie cutters came out, there were just a few choices in the metal categories. Now in metal and colorful plastic, there are shapes for virtually everything. There are collectors who seek out old varieties and new shapes. Cut-out cookies allow for creating specific shapes to be designed for special events or to tell a story. If you aren't going to frost the cookies, you can decorate with sprinkles, nonpareils or colorful sugars before baking. If you are going to frost them, cool the

cut-out cookies before frosting with a favorite powdered sugar recipe or Royal Icing.

Beautiful Bar Cookies

Bar cookies can dress up a cookie platter, and they can offer a "cut above" on the choice selection. They are dense and moist...a little bit cake-like in their texture. Their batter or dough is pressed or poured into a baking pan. When cool they are cut into squares, triangles, or rectangles. They can be frosted or sprinkled with powdered sugar. Bars are so versatile and encompass so many classic flavors. Take your pick from Pumpkin Spice Bars with cream cheese frosting, Lemon Chess Bars, Luscious Banana Bars and Apricot-Layer Bars.

Holiday & Party Cookies

Thanksgiving has its turkey, and Easter has its ham. But if we had to pick a quintessential food for Christmas, we would have to insist on cookies. No matter your ethnicity, there are family cookie favorites that must be made each holiday season. Is it Candy Cane Thumbprints, Big Crunchy Sugar Cookies or Fruitcake Bars that has to be on the list each year? In an effort to ease up on holiday time constraints, many cookie bakers team up to host or go to a cookie exchange. Bake a lot of one kind of cookie, take it to the party and exchange some of your cookies with those of others. Everyone goes home with a delightful mixture of sweet treats. But even though Christmas is certainly in first place for cookie baking, Halloween has become another favorite party holiday that lends itself to great cookie fun. Try making some Witches' Brooms cookies or perhaps Spiderweb Cookies for that spooky party. Any holiday or party is better with homemade cookies, and when the happy event is over, it is fun to share whatever goodies are left with family & friends.

Sugar-Topped Cookies, p. 18

CHAPTER ONE

Rolled & Shaped Cookies

Nanny's Peanut Butter Goblins, p. 30

Pecan Cookie Balls, p. 14

Mel Chencharick, Julian, PA

Ice Cream Nut Roll Crescents

Vanilla ice cream makes these cookies so rich and delicious.

Makes 4 dozen

4 c. all-purpose flour
2 c. butter, softened
1 pt. vanilla ice cream, softened
3/4 c. milk
2 8-oz. pkgs. walnuts, finely chopped
1 c. sugar
1 t. vanilla extract
Garnish: powdered sugar

Combine flour, butter and ice cream in a large bowl; mix well. Form dough into 4 balls; wrap in plastic wrap and refrigerate for 8 hours. In a saucepan, heat milk just to boiling; pour into a bowl and let cool slightly. To milk, add walnuts, sugar and vanilla; stir in a little more milk if too thick. Turn out one chilled dough ball onto a powdered sugar-covered surface. Roll out dough into a circle, 1/8-inch thick. With a pizza cutter, cut circle into 12 wedges. Spread 2 teaspoons walnut mixture onto each wedge; don't overfill. Starting on the wide end, roll up each wedge and form into a crescent shape. Arrange cookies on ungreased baking sheets. Repeat with remaining dough balls. Bake at 350 degrees for 18 to 20 minutes. Sprinkle with powdered sugar while still warm. Let cool. Store in an airtight container.

Nichole Wrigley, Vancouver, WA

Mom & Me Peanut Butter Kisses

My mom and I first made these for the holidays...but they were so good that we make them year 'round now!

Makes about 2 dozen

1 c. creamy peanut butter
1 c. sugar
1 egg, beaten
24 milk chocolate drops, unwrapped

Combine peanut butter, sugar and egg in a bowl; mix well. Roll into small balls and arrange on an ungreased baking sheet. Bake at 350 degrees for 12 minutes. Remove from oven; immediately place a chocolate drop in the center of each cookie. Cool completely.

Mom & Me Peanut Butter Kisses

April Hale, Kirkwood, NY

Buttery Ricotta Cookies

Who would have thought that ricotta cheese could make a cookie so yummy?

Makes about 2 dozen

1/2 c. butter, softened
1/4 c. ricotta cheese
1 c. sugar
1 egg, beaten
1 t. vanilla extract
2 c. all-purpose flour
1/2 t. baking soda
1/2 t. salt

Beat butter and ricotta cheese in a large bowl with an electric mixer at medium speed until creamy. Gradually add sugar, beating until blended; stir in egg and vanilla. Add remaining ingredients, stirring to blend. Shape dough into one-inch balls and flatten slightly on greased baking sheets. Bake at 350 degrees for 10 minutes, or until edges are golden. Remove to wire racks to cool. Store in an airtight container.

COOKIE KNOW-HOW
It is best not to overmix cookie dough. It can make the cookies a bit tougher and not so chewy.

Mary Sewell, Milford, CT

Molasses Sugar Cookies

When I bake these cookies, the smell reminds me of when my children were little. When they came home from school and realized I'd made them, they would jump for joy!

Makes about 4 dozen

3/4 c. shortening
1 c. sugar
1/4 c. molasses
1 egg, beaten
2 c. all-purpose flour
2 t. baking soda
1 t. cinnamon
1/2 t. ground cloves
1/2 t. ground ginger
1/2 t. salt
Garnish: additional sugar

Melt shortening in a small saucepan over medium heat; pour into a large mixing bowl and cool. Add sugar, molasses and egg. Beat well. Sift together flour, baking soda, spices and salt in a separate bowl. Stir into molasses mixture. Chill 4 hours. Form into one-inch balls and roll in additional sugar. Place on greased baking sheets. Bake at 375 degrees for 8 to 10 minutes.

Molasses Sugar Cookies

Sherry Gordon, Arlington Heights, IL

Peanut Butter Surprise Cookies

Yum, yum, yum! I like to divvy up the dough between baking sheets and chill the second batch while the first is baking.

Makes one dozen

16-1/2 oz. tube refrigerated peanut
   butter cookie dough
12 mini peanut butter cups
1/3 c. semi-sweet chocolate chips
1 t. shortening

Divide cookie dough into 12 pieces. With floured fingers, wrap one piece of dough around each peanut butter cup. Place on ungreased baking sheets. Bake at 350 degrees for 10 to 15 minutes, until golden. Cool on baking sheets one minute; remove to wire rack to cool completely. In a saucepan, melt chocolate chips and shortening over low heat, stirring constantly. Drizzle melted chocolate over cookies. Let stand until set.

Jodi Eisenhooth, McVeytown, PA

Pecan Cookie Balls

Make these sweet, crisp little morsels to go with an after-dinner cup of tea or coffee.

Makes 2-1/2 to 3 dozen

1 c. butter, softened
1 c. powdered sugar
2 c. chopped pecans
1 T. vanilla extract
2 c. all-purpose flour
4 T. powdered sugar

Blend together butter and powdered sugar; add pecans, vanilla and flour. Wrap dough in plastic wrap; chill for about 3 hours. Form dough into 3/4-inch balls; place on ungreased baking sheets. Bake at 350 degrees for 10 minutes. Let cool; roll in powdered sugar.

Pecan Cookie Balls

Virginia Cook, Fairfield, CT

Twist Cookies

So pretty on a tea tray. Sprinkle with colored sugar for extra sparkle.

Makes about 5 dozen

1 c. butter, softened
1-1/2 c. sugar
6 eggs, divided
1 t. vanilla extract
4 t. baking powder
4 to 5 c. all-purpose flour
Optional: sanding sugar

In a large bowl, beat butter with an electric mixer on high speed until fluffy, 4 to 5 minutes. Gradually add sugar, beating another 5 minutes. Add 4 eggs, one at a time, beating well after each addition. Blend in vanilla and baking powder. Gradually stir in flour until a stiff dough forms. Roll dough into one-inch balls. Roll each ball into an 8-inch long rope; fold in half and twist 2 to 3 times. Place on aluminum foil-lined baking sheets; set aside. Beat remaining eggs; brush over twists. Sprinkle with sugar, if using. Bake at 350 degrees for 15 to 20 minutes.

Holly Child, Parker, CO

Cherry-Cardamom Cookies

These cookies are so tasty!

Makes about 3 dozen

6-oz. jar maraschino cherries, drained and diced
2-1/3 c. plus 2 T. all-purpose flour, divided
1 t. baking powder
1 t. cardamom
1/2 t. baking soda
1/2 c. butter, softened
1 c. sugar
3-oz. pkg. cream cheese, softened
1 egg, beaten
2 T. buttermilk
1 t. almond extract
Garnish: powdered sugar

Combine cherries and 2 tablespoons flour in a small bowl. Toss to mix; set aside. Combine remaining flour, baking powder, cardamom and baking soda in a medium bowl, stirring to mix. Beat butter, sugar and cream cheese in a large bowl with an electric mixer at medium speed until fluffy. Add egg, buttermilk and almond extract; beat until blended. Gradually add flour mixture to butter mixture, beating just until moistened; fold in cherry mixture. Chill for one hour. Shape dough into one-inch balls; place on ungreased baking sheets. Bake at 350 degrees for 12 to 14 minutes; remove to wire racks to cool completely. Garnish with powdered sugar. Store in an airtight container.

Cherry Cardamom Cookies

Dee Ann Ice, Delaware, OH

Raspberry-Almond Shortbread Cookies

These buttery-delicious cookies look beautiful on a cookie tray!

Makes 3-1/2 dozen

1 c. butter, softened
2/3 c. sugar
1 t. almond extract
2 c. all-purpose flour
1/2 c. seedless raspberry jam
1 c. powdered sugar
2 to 3 t. water

Combine butter, sugar and almond extract in a large bowl. Beat with an electric mixer on medium speed until creamy. Reduce speed to low; gradually beat in flour until well mixed. Shape dough into one-inch balls. Place on ungreased baking sheets, 2 inches apart. Gently press a thumbprint into the center of each ball. Fill each with 1/4 teaspoon jam. Bake at 350 degrees for 14 to 18 minutes, until edges are lightly golden. Let cool one minute on baking sheet; remove to wire racks to cool completely. In a separate bowl, combine powdered sugar and water; stir well and drizzle lightly over cookies.

Lizzy Burnley, Ankeny, IA

Sugar-Topped Cookies

Everyone needs a dependable sugar cookie recipe...this is mine. These are quick and my boys love them. The sugar on top makes them so yummy!

Makes 2 dozen

1 c. butter, softened
1-1/4 c. sugar
1 egg, beaten
2 T. oil
1 T. milk
1 t. vanilla extract
1/2 t. almond extract
2-3/4 c. all-purpose flour
1 t. baking powder
1/2 t. baking soda
1/2 t. salt
1/4 c. water for dipping
3 T. sugar for dipping

In a large bowl, blend butter and sugar together; stir in egg, oil, milk, vanilla and almond extract. In another bowl mix flour, baking powder, baking soda and salt. Add flour mixture to butter mixture and mix until well blended. Shape dough into a ball; chill in freezer for 10 minutes. Shape into 1-1/2 inch balls and dip in water and sugar. Place on parchment paper-lined baking sheets and press down with fork. Sprinkle with sugar again. Bake at 350 degrees for 8 to 10 minutes, until golden. Cool on wire racks.

Sugar-Topped Cookies

Thais Menges, Three Rivers, MI

Grandma Miller's Nutmeg Logs

You'll want more than just one!

Makes 4 dozen

1 c. butter, softened
3/4 c. sugar
1 egg, slightly beaten
2 t. vanilla extract
2 t. rum extract
1 t. nutmeg
3 c. all-purpose flour
Garnish: additional nutmeg

In a large bowl, blend together butter and sugar. Stir in egg and extracts. Add nutmeg and flour; mix well. Divide dough into 4 portions. Roll each portion into a long rope; cut into 1-1/2 inch lengths. Place on ungreased baking sheets. Bake at 350 degrees for 10 to 15 minutes. Cool on wire racks. Spread Frosting on cookies. Run the tines of a fork across frosting to resemble a log. Sprinkle lightly with nutmeg.

Frosting:
3 T. butter, softened
1/2 t. vanilla extract
1 t. rum extract
2-1/2 c. powdered sugar
3 T. milk

Combine butter, extracts and powdered sugar. Blend in milk to desired consistency.

Shawna Brock, Eglin AFB, FL

White Chocolate-Cranberry Cookies

Dried cranberries and white chocolate make these cookies the best!

Makes 2-1/2 dozen

1/2 c. butter, softened
3/4 c. sugar
1/2 c. brown sugar, packed
1 egg, beaten
1 t. vanilla extract
1-3/4 c. all-purpose flour
1 t. baking powder
1/2 t. baking soda
1 c. sweetened dried cranberries
1/2 c. white chocolate chips

Beat butter in a large bowl at medium speed with an electric mixer until creamy; gradually add sugars, beating until combined. Add egg and vanilla; beat until smooth. Combine flour, baking powder and baking soda; gradually add to sugar mixture, beating well. Stir in cranberries and chocolate chips. Shape dough into 1-1/2 inch balls; place 2 inches apart on ungreased baking sheets. Bake at 375 degrees for 14 minutes or until golden. Remove to wire racks to cool.

White Chocolate-Cranberry Cookies

Amy Love, Delaware, OH

Snickerdoodles

The kids in my son's class asked for these cookies whenever there was a special event at school...he always brought home an empty container!

Makes 4-1/2 dozen

1-1/2 c. plus 2 T. sugar, divided
1/2 c. butter, softened
2 eggs, beaten
1 t. vanilla extract
2-3/4 c. all-purpose flour
1 t. cream of tartar
1/2 t. baking soda
1/2 t. salt
2 t. cinnamon

Blend 1-1/2 cups sugar, butter, eggs and vanilla in a large bowl. Add flour, cream of tartar, baking soda and salt; mix well. Form into one-inch balls. In a small bowl, mix together cinnamon and remaining sugar. Roll balls in cinnamon-sugar; place on parchment paper-lined baking sheets. Bake at 400 degrees for 8 minutes. Immediately remove to a wire rack to cool.

Lisa Ashton, Aston, PA

Cinnamon Gingersnaps

These simple, spicy-sweet cookies are so nice for dipping into a cup of hot coffee or herbal tea.

Makes 4 dozen

3/4 c. butter, softened
1 c. brown sugar, packed
1 egg, beaten
1/4 c. molasses
2-1/4 c. all-purpose flour
2 t. baking soda
1/2 t. salt
2 t. cinnamon
1 t. ground ginger
1/2 to 1 c. sugar

Blend together butter and brown sugar in a large bowl. Stir in egg and molasses; set aside. In a separate bowl, combine flour, baking soda, salt and spices. Gradually add flour mixture to butter mixture; mix well. Roll dough into one-inch balls; roll in sugar. Arrange on parchment paper-lined baking sheets, 2 inches apart. Bake at 350 degrees for 10 to 12 minutes, until cookies are set and tops are cracked. Remove to wire racks; cool completely.

Cinnamon Gingersnaps

Brenda Huey, Geneva, IN

Lemon Snowdrops

These pretty cookies are so good...
they melt in your mouth!

Makes 4 to 6 dozen

2 c. plus 3 T. shortening, divided
1 c. powdered sugar
2 t. lemon extract
1/2 t. salt
4 c. all-purpose flour
2 eggs, beaten
juice and zest of 1 lemon
1-1/3 c. sugar
Garnish: powdered sugar

Mix together 2 cups shortening, powdered sugar, lemon extract and salt; slowly stir in flour until blended. Roll dough into one-inch balls and arrange on ungreased baking sheets. Press a thumbprint into the center of each ball; set aside. In a large saucepan, combine remaining ingredients except garnish. Cook and stir over low heat until slightly thickened. Spoon one teaspoon filling into each thumbprint. Bake at 325 degrees for 8 to 10 minutes, until lightly golden. Let cool; dust with powdered sugar.

Carol Field Dahlstrom, Ankeny, IA

Fudgy Cappuccino Crinkles

These cookies are so chocolatey and good...and pretty too!

Makes about 3 dozen

3/4 c. butter, softened
3 T. oil
1 c. brown sugar, packed
2/3 c. baking cocoa
1 T. instant coffee granules
1 t. baking soda
1 t. cinnamon
2 egg whites
1/4 c. vanilla low-fat yogurt
1-1/2 c. all-purpose flour
1/4 to 1/2 c. powdered sugar, sifted

Beat butter with an electric mixer on medium speed 30 seconds. Add oil, brown sugar, cocoa, coffee granules, baking soda and cinnamon. Beat until combined, scraping bowl. Beat in egg whites and yogurt until combined. Beat in as much flour as you can. Stir in any remaining flour. Place powdered sugar in a small bowl. Roll into 1-inch balls and roll in powdered sugar. Place 2 inches apart on lightly greased baking sheets. Bake at 350 degrees for 8 to 10 minutes or until edges are firm. Transfer to a wire rack and let cool.

Fudgy Cappuccino Crinkles

Maria Jones, Tampa, FL

Cinnamon-Sugar Butter Cookies

These tasty cookies can be made ahead and frozen for up to one month.

Makes 3 dozen

2-1/2 c. all-purpose flour
1/2 t. baking soda
1/4 t. salt
1 c. brown sugar, packed
1/2 c. plus 3 T. sugar, divided
1 c. butter, softened
2 eggs, beaten
2 t. vanilla extract
1 T. cinnamon

Combine flour, baking soda and salt in a bowl; mix well and set aside. Combine brown sugar and 1/2 cup sugar in a separate bowl; mix well. Add butter and beat with an electric mixer at medium speed until well blended. Add eggs and vanilla; beat 2 minutes, or until fluffy. Add flour mixture and stir just until blended. Refrigerate dough 30 minutes, or until firm. Shape dough into one-inch balls. Combine remaining sugar and cinnamon in a shallow bowl and mix well; roll balls in cinnamon-sugar mixture. Place 2 inches apart on ungreased baking sheets. Bake at 300 degrees for 18 to 20 minutes. Remove from baking sheets; cool on wire racks.

Beckie Butcher, Elgin, IL

Grandma's Pecan Balls

Include this old-fashioned classic on any cookie tray. They will love them!

Makes about 2 dozen cookies

1 c. butter, softened
1/3 c. sugar
2 t. vanilla extract
2 c. all-purpose flour
2 c. chopped pecans
Garnish: powdered sugar

In a medium bowl, blend together butter and sugar; stir in vanilla and flour. Stir in pecans. Roll dough into walnut-size balls, and arrange on ungreased baking sheets. Bake at 325 degrees for 45 minutes. While still warm, sprinkle cookies with powdered sugar; sprinkle again before serving.

Grandma's Pecan Balls

Shawna Green, Dumas, TX

Pistachio Thumbprints

Everyone raves about these delicious cookies!

Makes 3 dozen

1 c. butter, softened
1/3 c. powdered sugar
1 egg, beaten
1 t. vanilla extract
3/4 t. almond extract
2 c. all-purpose flour
3.4-oz. pkg. instant pistachio
    pudding mix
1 c. pecans, finely chopped
1/2 c. semi-sweet chocolate chips
2 t. shortening

In a large bowl, blend butter, powdered sugar, egg and extracts. Stir in flour and dry pudding mix. Form dough into one-inch balls; roll in pecans. Place on greased baking sheets; gently press a thumbprint into each. Bake at 350 degrees for 10 to 12 minutes; let cool. Spoon Vanilla Filling into thumbprints. In a plastic zipping bag, microwave chocolate chips and shortening until melted, one to 2 minutes, stirring every 15 seconds. Snip off the tip of one corner; drizzle over cookies.

Vanilla Filling:
2 T. butter, softened
2 c. powdered sugar
1 t. vanilla extract
2 T. milk

Combine all ingredients; mix well.

Dayna Hale, Galena, OH

Favorite Sugar Cookies

Oh-so soft and sugary...just what a sugar cookie should be! Try rolling the cookies in colored sanding sugars for a fun surprise for the kids. Then serve the cookies with strawberry-flavored milk to top it off!

Makes 4 dozen

1 c. shortening
2 c. sugar
2 eggs, beaten
2 t. vanilla extract
2 t. baking powder
1/2 t. baking soda
1 t. salt
4 c. all-purpose flour
1 c. milk
Garnish: additional sugar

Beat together shortening and sugar. Add eggs and vanilla; set aside. In a separate bowl, combine baking powder, baking soda, salt and flour; add to shortening mixture alternately with milk, beating well. Chill dough one to 2 hours. Roll into balls and then into sugar. Place on greased baking sheets. Bake at 350 degrees for 8 to 10 minutes.

Favorite Sugar Cookies

Holly Child, Parker, CO

Cranberry & Sugar Sandies

This makes such a pretty cookie with the dried cranberries peeking through the powdered sugar.

Makes 2 to 3 dozen

1 c. butter
1-1/2 c. powdered sugar, divided
1 t. vanilla extract
2-1/4 c. all-purpose flour
1/4 t. salt
1/2 c. dried cranberries
Optional: 3/4 c. chopped walnuts

Beat butter, 1/2 cup powdered sugar and vanilla in a large bowl with an electric mixer at medium speed until creamy. Gradually add flour, salt, dried cranberries and nuts, if desired; mix well. Shape dough into one-inch balls and place on ungreased baking sheets. Bake at 400 degrees for 10 to 12 minutes. Place remaining powdered sugar in a bowl. Roll warm cookies in powdered sugar; let cool completely and roll again.

> **COOKIE KNOW-HOW**
> For best results, be sure to use the type of fat named in the recipe. Butter bakes up well and gives cookies wonderful flavor. Avoid light or whipped butters when baking. If shortening is called for, look for it in easy-to-measure sticks.

Beverly Mahorney, Cynthiana, KY

Nanny's Peanut Butter Goblins

My mom made these every year when she hosted a fall open house. They are simple and scrumptious! Now when I make her cookies, I feel like she's still with us.

Makes 3 dozen

1/2 c. butter, softened
1 c. crunchy peanut butter
1/2 c. brown sugar, packed
1 c. sugar, divided
1 egg, beaten
1 t. vanilla extract
1-1/2 c. all-purpose flour
1/2 t. baking soda
1/2 t. salt

In a large bowl, combine butter, peanut butter, brown sugar and 1/2 cup sugar. Beat with an electric mixer on medium speed until blended; stir in egg and vanilla. In a separate bowl, mix together flour, baking soda and salt. Add flour mixture to butter mixture; stir until a stiff dough forms. Roll dough into balls by tablespoonfuls. Roll balls in remaining sugar; place on greased baking sheets, 2 inches apart. With a fork dipped in sugar, flatten balls in a criss-cross pattern. Bake at 375 degrees for 10 to 12 minutes, until golden.

Nanny's Peanut Butter Goblins

Nina Jones, Springfield, OH

Apple Crisp Cookies

This recipe won the "Best Cookie in the County" prize for me at the Clark County Fair in Springfield, Ohio.

Makes 3 dozen

1 c. butter-flavored shortening
1 c. brown sugar, packed
2 t. vanilla extract
2-1/2 c. old-fashioned oats, uncooked
2-1/4 c. all-purpose flour
1/2 t. baking soda
1/2 t. salt
1/2 c. water
1 t. cinnamon
1/4 c. sugar
21-oz. can apple pie filling, finely chopped

Combine shortening, brown sugar and vanilla in a large bowl. Beat with an electric mixer on medium speed until well blended. In a separate bowl, combine oats, flour, baking soda and salt. Add oat mixture alternately with water to shortening mixture; stir until well blended. Combine cinnamon and sugar in a small bowl. Reserve one cup of dough for topping. Shape remaining dough into one-inch balls. Roll each ball in cinnamon-sugar; place on parchment paper-lined baking sheets, 2 inches apart. Flatten each ball with the bottom of a cup coated with cinnamon-sugar. Bake at 375 degrees for 6 minutes. Remove from oven; cool for 5 minutes. Top each cookie with a dollop of pie filling and a sprinkle of Crumb Topping. Bake another 5 minutes. Cool slightly; remove to wire racks.

Crumb Topping:
1 c. reserved cookie dough
1/4 c. old-fashioned oats, uncooked
1/2 t. cinnamon
2 T. brown sugar, packed
1/2 c. finely chopped pecans

Mix reserved dough with remaining ingredients until a crumbly mixture forms.

Karen Harris, Delaware, OH

Butterscotch Cookies

A nice twist with butterscotch chips!

Makes 5 dozen

1/2 c. butter, softened
3/4 c. sugar
3/4 c. brown sugar, packed
2 eggs, beaten
1 t. vanilla extract
1-1/2 c. all-purpose flour
1 t. salt
1 t. baking soda
12-oz. pkg. butterscotch chips
6-oz. pkg. toffee baking bits
1 c. chopped pecans

Blend butter and sugars in a large bowl. Add eggs and vanilla; mix well and set aside. In a separate bowl, mix flour, salt and baking soda. Stir flour mixture into sugar mixture. Fold in chips, toffee bits and pecans. Cover and chill dough at least 30 minutes. Roll dough into 1-1/2 inch balls. Place on ungreased baking sheets, 2 inches apart. Bake at 325 degrees for 9 to 12 minutes. Cool on wire racks.

Butterscotch Cookies

Pretty Swirl Cookies, p. 50

CHAPTER TWO

Easy Icebox & No-Bake Cookies

No-Bake Granola Bars, p. 46

Key Lime Bites, p. 42

Henry Burnley, Ankeny, IA

Chocolate Almond Oatmeal Cookies

I am only 10 years old, but I can make these by myself because you don't have to bake them!

Makes about 2 dozen

1/3 c. butter, melted
1-1/2 c. sugar
1/2 c. milk
1/3 c. baking cocoa
1/2 c. creamy almond butter
3 c. old-fashioned oats, uncooked

In a saucepan over medium heat, combine butter, sugar, milk and cocoa. Bring to a boil; cook for one minute. Remove from heat; stir in remaining ingredients. Mix well; drop by rounded teaspoonfuls onto wax paper. Let cookies cool completely.

Judy Gillham, Whittier, CA

Spicy Maple-Anise Snaps

This old-fashioned German icebox cookie is a much-requested family favorite. It even won me a ribbon at the Los Angeles County Fair. The delicious blending of anise and maple in this treat really pleases.

Makes 7 dozen

1 c. butter, softened
1 c. sugar
1 c. dark brown sugar, packed
1 egg, beaten
1 t. maple extract
2-1/2 c. all-purpose flour
1 T. ground anise seed
1 t. baking soda
1 t. cinnamon
3/4 t. ground cloves
1/2 c. pecans, finely chopped

In a large bowl, beat butter and sugars with an electric mixer at medium speed, until fluffy. Beat in egg and extract; set aside. Combine flour and remaining ingredients except nuts in a separate bowl; mix well. Gradually blend flour mixture into butter mixture; beat at low speed until blended. Add pecans and mix in well. Divide dough into 3 parts; form each into a log 8 inches long. Wrap tightly in wax paper; chill one hour, or until very firm. Remove one roll at a time from refrigerator and slice 1/4-inch thick. Place slices one to 2 inches apart on parchment paper-lined baking sheets. Bake at 375 degrees for 10 to 12 minutes, until golden. Immediately remove cookies from baking sheets; cool completely on wire racks. Store in airtight containers. Flavors will become more pronounced over the next several days.

Spicy Maple-Anise Snaps

Hope Davenport, Portland, TX

Snowballs

Covered in coconut flakes...there'll be no snowball fights with these!

Makes about 2 dozen

1 c. semi-sweet chocolate chips
1/3 c. evaporated milk
1 c. powdered sugar
1/2 c. chopped walnuts
1-1/4 c. sweetened flaked coconut

Combine chocolate chips and milk in a double boiler; cook over hot water until chocolate melts. Stir to blend well. Remove from heat; stir in powdered sugar and nuts. Cool slightly. Form into one-inch balls; roll in coconut.

Kendall Hale, Lynn, MA

Lemon Slice Cookies

These also make a great gift! Package them in little cellophane bags and tie them with a ribbon.

Makes about 3 dozen

1 c. butter, softened
1 c. brown sugar, packed
1/2 c. sugar
1 egg, beaten
1 T. lemon zest
2 T. lemon juice
2 c. all-purpose flour
1/4 t. baking soda
1/2 t. salt
Optional: powdered sugar

Beat butter and sugars until light and fluffy; blend in egg, lemon zest and lemon juice. In a separate bowl, combine flour, baking soda and salt; add to butter mixture and mix until just blended. Divide dough in half; with floured hands, shape each half into a 10-inch long log. Wrap each in plastic wrap; refrigerate until firm. Cut each roll into 1/4-inch thick slices; arrange on greased baking sheets. Bake at 400 degrees for 8 to 10 minutes; cool on a wire rack. Dust with powdered sugar if desired.

Lemon Slice Cookies

Lori Hobscheidt, Washington, IA

Cale's Corn Flake Cookies

Sweet, crunchy and peanut buttery! An easy no-bake recipe using pantry staples.

Makes 4 dozen

1 c. light corn syrup
1 c. creamy peanut butter
1 c. sugar
1 t. vanilla extract
6 to 7 c. corn flake cereal

Combine all ingredients except cereal in a large heavy saucepan; cook and stir over low heat until sugar dissolves. Add cereal; stir well and drop by tablespoonfuls onto wax paper. Let stand until set.

Lyne Neymeyer, Des Moines, IA

Almond Butter Slices

These buttery bites are delicious!

Makes 2-1/2 dozen

1 c. plus 2 T. butter, softened and
   divided
1/2 c. almond butter
1/2 c. brown sugar, packed
1/2 t. almond extract
2 c. all-purpose flour
3 T. cornstarch
1/4 t. salt
8 sqs. bittersweet baking chocolate,
   chopped
Optional: chocolate sprinkles

In a large bowl, beat one cup butter, almond butter, brown sugar and extract with an electric mixer on medium speed until well combined. In a medium bowl stir together flour, cornstarch and salt. Gradually add flour mixture to butter mixture, beating on low until combined. Divide dough in half. Form each half into a square log shape. Wrap each half in plastic wrap and refrigerate for 2 hours or overnight. Slice into 1/2-inch thick slices and place one inch apart on ungreased baking sheets. Repeat with remaining dough. Bake at 300 degrees for 12 to 15 minutes, until lightly golden. Remove; cool on wire racks. In a small bowl combine chocolate and remaining butter. Microwave at 30-second intervals, stirring after each, until chocolate is melted. Dip corner of each cookie into chocolate, allowing excess to drip off. Place on parchment paper or wax paper. Decorate as desired.

Almond Butter Slices

Beth Kramer, Port Saint Lucie, FL

Chocolate-Orange Snowballs

Vanilla wafers are the secret to these simple, no-bake cookie favorite.

Makes 5 dozen

9-oz. pkg. vanilla wafers
1-1/4 c. powdered sugar, divided
1/4 c. baking cocoa
1/3 c. light corn syrup
1/3 c. frozen orange juice
    concentrate, thawed
1-1/2 c. chopped pecans

In a food processor, combine vanilla wafers, one cup powdered sugar, cocoa, corn syrup and orange juice. Process until wafers are finely ground and mixture is well blended. Add pecans and process until nuts are finely chopped. Transfer mixture to a bowl; form into one-inch balls. Roll in remaining powdered sugar. Store in an airtight container.

Jan Temeyer, Ankeny, IA

Key Lime Bites

A little food coloring and a twist of lime makes these sliced cookies a refreshing favorite.

Makes 2 dozen

3/4 c. butter, softened
1 c. powdered sugar, divided
zest of 2 limes
2 T. lime juice
1 T. vanilla extract
1-3/4 c. plus 2 T. all-purpose flour
2 T. cornstarch
1/2 t. salt
Optional: few drops green food
    coloring
Garnish: lime zest curls

Beat butter and 1/3 cup powdered sugar in a large bowl with an electric mixer at medium speed until fluffy. Add zest, lime juice and vanilla; beat until blended. Whisk together flour, cornstarch and salt in a separate bowl; add flour mixture to butter mixture, stirring until combined. Add food coloring if desired. Shape dough into a log and chill one hour. Cut log into 1/8-inch thick slices; place on parchment paper-lined baking sheets. Bake at 350 degrees for 12 to 14 minutes, until golden. Remove to wire racks and cool. Frost with Simple Frosting and top with lime curls.

Simple Frosting:
2 c. powdered sugar
1 T. butter, melted
2 T. milk

Mix all ingredients together until smooth.

Key Lime Bites

Emily Puskac, New Cumberland, WV

Hazelnut Pinwheels

For the neatest slices, use dental floss to cut the dough. Position it under the roll, bring up the floss ends, cross over the center and gently pull to cut the slices...easy!

Makes about 2 dozen

1 c. butter, softened
1 c. sugar
2 egg yolks, beaten
1 t. vanilla extract
1 t. orange extract
1 t. orange zest
2 c. all-purpose flour
1/2 chocolate-hazelnut spread, divided

In a large bowl, blend butter and sugar until creamy. Stir in egg yolks and extracts. Add orange zest and flour; mix well. Cover and refrigerate dough for 30 minutes. Divide dough into 2 balls. On a floured surface, roll out one ball into a rectangle, 1/4-inch thick. Spread with half of the chocolate-hazelnut spread, leaving a 1/4-inch border. Roll up dough jelly-roll style. Repeat with remaining dough and spread. Refrigerate another 30 minutes. Slice rolls 1/2-inch thick. Arrange slices on an ungreased baking sheet. Bake at 350 degrees for 12 to 15 minutes, or until edges are slightly golden. Cool on wire racks.

Lynn Williams, Muncie, IN

Dazzling Neapolitan Cookies

The star of the cookie plate!

Makes 8 dozen

1 c. butter, softened
1 c. sugar
1 egg, beaten
1 t. vanilla extract
2-1/2 c. all-purpose flour
1-1/2 t. baking powder
1/2 t. salt
1-oz. sq. semi-sweet baking chocolate, melted
1/3 c. chopped pecans
1/4 c. candied cherries, diced
2 drops red food coloring
1/3 c. flaked coconut
1/2 t. almond extract

In a large bowl, combine butter and sugar. Beat with an electric mixer at medium speed until light and fluffy; add egg and vanilla, beating until blended. Gradually beat in flour, baking powder and salt. Divide dough into thirds. Stir chocolate and pecans into one third, cherries and food coloring into another third and coconut and almond extract into remaining third. Line an 8"x8" baking pan with plastic wrap, allowing 2 inches to extend over sides; press chocolate mixture evenly into bottom of pan. Add coconut mixture and then cherry mixture, gently pressing each layer; cover and chill 8 hours. Lift dough from pan; cut into 5 equal sections. Carefully cut each section into 1/8-inch thick slices; place on ungreased baking sheets. Bake at 375 degrees for 8 to 10 minutes, until golden; remove to wire racks to cool.

Dazzling Neapolitan Cookies

Mary Ann Saint, Indian Land, SC

Grandma Saint's Fridge Cookies

My sister-in-law in Louisiana always made these cookies for us when we visited. She knew my husband would be so happy to eat the cookies his mother used to make. In fact, it made all of us happy...they're the most delicious refrigerator cookies I've ever tasted. You can't eat just one... they are addictive!

Makes 4 dozen

1 c. butter, softened
1 c. light brown sugar, packed
1 egg, beaten
1 t. vanilla extract
2 c. all-purpose flour
1/2 t. baking soda
1/4 t. salt
1 c. chopped pecans

In a large bowl, blend butter and sugar. Add egg and vanilla; mix well. In a separate bowl, mix together remaining ingredients except pecans. Add flour mixture to butter mixture and stir well; add pecans. Divide dough into 2 parts. Form each part into a roll; wrap rolls in wax paper. Refrigerate at least 2 hours to overnight. Cut dough into 1/2-inch thick slices; arrange 2 inches apart on lightly greased or parchment paper-lined baking sheets. Bake at 350 degrees for 14 to 15 minutes.

Patrice Lindsey, Lockport, IL

No-Bake Granola Bars

These are perfect bars to pack in the kids' lunches or for a quick-grab breakfast.

Makes 16 bars

1/4 c. coconut oil, divided
1 c. creamy peanut butter
1/2 c. honey
2 c. long-cooking oats, uncooked
2 c. crispy rice cereal
1 c. sweetened flaked coconut
1/2 c. dried cranberries, chopped
1/2 c. mini semi-sweet chocolate
   chips

Lightly grease a 13"x9" baking pan with a small amount of coconut oil; set aside. In a large saucepan, combine remaining coconut oil, peanut butter and honey. Cook and stir over low heat just until blended and smooth. Remove from heat; add oats, cereal, coconut and cranberries. Stir just until evenly coated and well combined. Let cool about 10 minutes; stir in chocolate chips. Quickly transfer mixture to baking pan; spread evenly with a spatula. Cover with plastic wrap or wax paper; press mixture down evenly and firmly. Refrigerate for one hour before cutting into bars. May be kept tightly covered and refrigerated for up to 10 days.

No-Bake Granola Bars

Leona Krivda, Belle Vernon, PA

No-Bake Yummy Balls

This is a yummy, quick toss-together snack. The grandkids really like them, and my hubby and I love them with a cup of coffee. And they are healthy!

Makes 2 dozen

1-1/2 c. sweetened flaked coconut, toasted and divided
1 c. quick-cooking oats, uncooked
1/2 c. creamy peanut butter
1/3 c. honey
1/4 c. ground flax seed
1/4 c. wheat germ
1/4 c. mini semi-sweet chocolate chips
1/4 c. chopped walnuts
2 T. dried cranberries or cherries, chopped
1 t. vanilla extract

Combine 2/3 cup coconut and remaining ingredients in a bowl. Mix well with your hands. If mixture is too dry, a little more honey or peanut butter may be added. Roll into one-inch balls, then roll in remaining coconut. Place in an airtight container; cover and keep chilled.

Eileen Blass, Catawissa, PA

Peanut Butter-Chocolate Bars

Top with marshmallow creme for s'more fun!

Makes 2 dozen

1 c. creamy peanut butter
1/2 c. butter, melted
1 c. graham cracker crumbs
16-oz. pkg. powdered sugar
2 c. semi-sweet chocolate chips, melted

Combine peanut butter, butter, graham cracker crumbs and powdered sugar together in a large mixing bowl; mix well using a wooden spoon. Press into the bottom of a well-greased 15"x10" jelly-roll pan; pour melted chocolate evenly over crust. Refrigerate mixture for 15 minutes; score into bars but leave in pan. Refrigerate until firm; slice completely through scores and serve cold.

Peanut Butter-Chocolate Bars

Angela Sims, Willow Springs, IL

No-Bake Peanut Butter Bars

With rich butterscotch frosting, these are no ordinary peanut butter bars...wow!

Makes 2 dozen

1-1/2 c. graham cracker crumbs
1 c. butter, melted
16-oz. pkg. powdered sugar
1 c. creamy peanut butter
12-oz. pkg. butterscotch chips

Combine first 4 ingredients together; mix well. Press into the bottom of a 13"x9" baking pan; set aside. Melt butterscotch chips in a double boiler; spread over crumb mixture. Refrigerate; cut into bars when cooled.

COOKIE KNOW-HOW
Spray your cup measure with non-stick vegetable spray and peanut butter will slide out easily when measuring.

Carol Field Dahlstrom, Ankeny, IA

Pretty Swirl Cookies

These look so special, but are easy to make because you mix them up, layer them, roll them and then slice them. Fun and pretty!

Makes 2 dozen

1 c. butter, softened
3/4 c. sugar
1/4 c. brown sugar, packed
1 egg, beaten
1 t. almond extract
2 c. all-purpose flour
1/2 t. baking powder
1/4 t. salt
few drops food coloring

In a large bowl, blend butter and sugars. Add egg and almond extract; mix well. Add flour, baking powder and salt to butter mixture and stir well. Divide dough into 2 parts. Color one part with red food coloring. Roll each part into an 8-inch by 6-inch rectangle. Layer the 2 pieces together. Roll up and wrap with parchment paper. Refrigerate at least two hours to overnight. Slice the dough into 1/2-inch thick slices; arrange slices 3 inches apart on parchment paper-lined baking sheets. Bake at 350 degrees for 14 to 15 minutes. Cool before removing from pan.

Pretty Swirl Cookies

Ann Heavey, Bridgewater, MA

Favorite Cocoa No-Bakes

A best-loved after-school snack for generations of kids.

Makes 2-1/2 to 3 dozen

3 c. quick-cooking oats, uncooked
2 c. sugar
1/2 c. butter, softened
1/2 c. milk
1/3 c. baking cocoa
2/3 c. creamy peanut butter
2 t. vanilla extract

Add oats to a blender and pulse until fine; set aside. Combine sugar, butter, milk and cocoa in a saucepan over medium heat. Bring to a rolling boil, stirring constantly. Remove from heat. Add peanut butter and vanilla; stir until smooth. Add oats and stir well. Let stand for 10 minutes. Drop by rounded tablespoonfuls onto aluminum foil-lined baking sheets; cool until set.

Michelle Tolmasoff, La Habra, CA

Hopscotch Cookies

Ever since my great-aunt discovered this recipe, we've enjoyed these no-bake cookies at family gatherings.

Makes 4 to 5 dozen

4 c. mini marshmallows
5-oz. can chow mein noodles
12-oz. pkg. butterscotch chips
1 c. creamy peanut butter

Combine marshmallows and noodles in a heatproof bowl; set aside. In a double boiler over medium heat, melt together butterscotch chips and peanut butter. Pour butterscotch mixture over marshmallow mixture. Stir until marshmallows are slightly melted. Drop by teaspoonfuls onto wax paper-lined baking sheets. Refrigerate at least 15 minutes before serving.

COOKIE KNOW-HOW
Using silicone parchment paper instead of greasing the baking sheet keeps cookies from becoming too brown on the bottom and makes clean up super easy.

Hopscotch Cookies

Carol Lytle, Columbus, OH

Mint-Chocolate Sandwiches

Crunchy, creamy, minty goodness...so yummy!

Makes 3 dozen

1/4 c. whipping cream
12-oz. pkg. semi-sweet chocolate
    chips, divided
3/4 t. peppermint extract
2 9-oz. pkgs. chocolate wafer cookies

In a saucepan, bring cream to a boil over medium-high heat. Add 3/4 cup chocolate chips; stir constantly until melted and smooth. Stir in extract. Remove from heat; let cool for 15 minutes. Spoon one teaspoon chocolate mixture onto a wafer cookie; sandwich with another cookie. Repeat with remaining cookies. Refrigerate for 10 minutes, or until firm. Meanwhile, in a microwave-safe bowl, microwave

remaining chocolate chips for one minute; stir until melted. Let cool slightly. Dip each sandwich into melted chocolate to coat; shake off excess. Place sandwiches on a wire rack set over a wax paper-lined baking sheet; refrigerate 15 minutes, or until set.

Lisa Langston, Conroe, TX

Graham No-Bake Cookies

A no-bake recipe that's a little different...I've never seen this version made with graham crackers anywhere else. We love them!

Makes 4 to 5 dozen

2 c. sugar
1/2 c. milk
2 T. baking cocoa
1/2 c. butter
1/2 c. creamy peanut butter
1 T. vanilla extract
2 c. quick-cooking oats, uncooked
1 c. graham cracker crumbs

Combine sugar, milk, cocoa and butter in a saucepan over medium heat. Bring to a boil and cook for 2 minutes, stirring constantly. Remove from heat. Stir in peanut butter, vanilla, oats and crumbs; mix well. Drop by rounded tablespoonfuls onto buttered wax paper; cool completely.

Graham No-Bake Cookies

Quarterback Crunch Brownies, p. 74

Brownies & Blondies

Rocky Road Bars, p. 62

Chocolate-Hazelnut Skillet Bars, p. 60

Naomi Cooper, Delaware, OH

Peanut Butter Brownies

A nice change of pace from chocolate brownies! Top with chocolate frosting for a whole new taste.

Makes 1-1/4 dozen

1 c. creamy peanut butter
1/2 c. butter, softened
2 c. brown sugar, packed
3 eggs, beaten
1 t. vanilla extract
1 c. all-purpose flour
1/2 t. salt

In a large bowl, blend together peanut butter and butter. Beat in brown sugar, eggs and vanilla until light and fluffy. Blend in flour and salt. Spread into a greased 13"x9" baking pan; bake at 350 degrees for 30 to 35 minutes. Cool in pan; frost with Peanut Butter Frosting.

Peanut Butter Frosting:
2 c. creamy peanut butter
1 c. butter, softened
1 t. vanilla extract
1/8 t. salt
3 to 4 T. whipping cream
2 c. powdered sugar

Blend peanut butter and butter until fluffy; gradually blend in remaining ingredients until smooth.

Brenda Ervin, Festus, MO

Fabulous Zucchini Brownies

The zucchini in these brownies keeps them moist.

Makes 20 brownies

1-1/4 c. sugar
1/3 c. oil
2 t. vanilla extract
2 c. all-purpose flour
1/2 c. baking cocoa
1 t. baking soda
2 c. zucchini, shredded
1/2 c. chopped pecans

Mix sugar, oil and vanilla; set aside. In a separate bowl, whisk together flour, cocoa, and baking soda. Blend in sugar mixture, zucchini and nuts. Pour into a lightly oiled 13"x9" baking pan and bake at 350 degrees for 25 to 30 minutes. Cut into squares.

Fabulous Zucchini Brownies

Heather Prentice, Mars, PA

Buckeye Brownies

Chocolate and peanut butter...these brownies taste just like our favorite buckeye candies!

Makes 2 to 3 dozen

19-1/2 oz. pkg. brownie mix
2 c. powdered sugar
1/2 c. plus 6 T. butter, softened and
   divided
1 c. creamy peanut butter
6-oz. pkg. semi-sweet chocolate
   chips

Prepare brownie mix according to package directions; bake in a greased 13"x9" baking pan. Let cool. Mix together powdered sugar, 1/2 cup butter and peanut butter; spread over cooled brownies. Chill for one hour. Melt together chocolate chips and remaining butter in a saucepan over low heat, stirring occasionally. Spread over brownies. Let cool; cut into squares.

COOKIE KNOW-HOW
Purchased brownie mixes are very tasty and can be used as a basis for fun brownie variations. Try adding 1/2 cup of dried cranberries, shredded coconut or candied orange peel to the mix and bake as directed.

Cheri Maxwell, Gulf Breeze, FL

Chocolate-Hazelnut Skillet Bars

These blondie-like bars are too good to pass up. If you aren't a fan of hazelnuts, try pecans, almonds or even peanuts...any of them would be just as tasty!

Serves 8

1-1/4 c. all-purpose flour
1/4 t. baking powder
1/2 t. baking soda
1/2 t. salt
1/2 c. butter
1 c. dark brown sugar, packed
1 egg, beaten
1-1/2 t. vanilla extract
1 t. espresso powder
3/4 c. dark baking chocolate, chopped
1/2 c. hazelnuts, chopped

In a bowl, combine flour, baking powder, baking soda and salt; set aside. Melt butter in a large cast-iron skillet over medium heat. Add brown sugar and whisk until sugar is dissolved, about one minute. Slowly pour butter mixture into flour mixture. Add egg, vanilla and espresso powder to flour mixture; stir until combined. Fold in remaining ingredients. Spoon dough into skillet; bake at 350 degrees for 20 to 25 minutes, until golden on top and a toothpick tests clean. Let stand 30 minutes; slice into wedges to serve.

Chocolate-Hazelnut Skillet Bars

Vickie, Gooseberry Patch

Brownie Buttons

Tell a best friend no one else can fill her shoes! Cover the lid of a plain shoe box with pictures of shoes cut from magazines or catalogs. Fill the box with homemade treats and wrap the box with pretty cotton string.

Makes 20

16-oz. pkg. refrigerated mini
    brownie bites dough
11-oz. pkg. assorted mini peanut
    butter cup candies and
    chocolate-coated caramels

Spray mini muffin cups with non-stick vegetable spray. Spoon brownie dough evenly into each cup, filling almost full. Bake at 350 degrees for 19 to 20 minutes. Cool in pans 3 to 4 minutes; gently press a candy into each baked brownie until top of candy is level with top of brownie. Cool 10 minutes in pans. Gently twist each brownie to remove from pan. Cool on a wire rack.

Dale-Harriet Rogovich, Madison, WI

Rocky Road Bars

Brownies, chocolate chips, marshmallows and peanuts... need I say more?

Makes 2 dozen

22-1/2 oz. pkg. brownie mix with
    chocolate syrup pouch
1/4 c. water
1/3 c. oil
2 eggs, beaten
12-oz. pkg. semi-sweet chocolate
    chips, divided
1-1/2 to 2 c. mini marshmallows
1-1/2 c. dry-roasted peanuts,
    chopped

Grease the bottom only of a 13"x9" baking pan; set aside. Combine brownie mix, syrup pouch, water, oil and eggs; stir until well blended. Mix in one cup chocolate chips; spread in baking pan. Bake at 350 degrees for 30 to 35 minutes, or until a toothpick inserted 2 inches from side of pan comes out clean. Immediately sprinkle with marshmallows, remaining chocolate chips and peanuts. Cover pan with a baking sheet for 2 to 3 minutes; remove and cool completely. Cut into bars; store tightly covered.

Rocky Road Bars

Linda Nichols, Wintersville, OH

Coconut-Pecan Fudge Brownies

Using a cake mix makes these brownies super easy to make.

Makes 2 dozen

15.25-oz. pkg. chocolate fudge
　　cake mix
15-oz. container coconut-pecan
　　frosting
1 c. applesauce
1 egg, beaten
Garnish: powdered sugar

Combine all ingredients except powdered sugar in a large bowl and mix well; spread in a lightly greased 13"x9" baking pan. Bake at 350 degrees for 30 to 32 minutes, until a toothpick inserted in center comes out clean. Cool for one hour; cut into 2-inch squares. Garnish with powdered sugar.

COOKIE KNOW-HOW
If you want to try a variation of a chocolate brownie, use a yellow cake mix instead of the fudge cake mix and you'll have a yummy blonde brownie.

Amy Gitter, Fond du Lac, WI

Double Chocolate-Mint Brownies

These fantastic brownies are rich and chocolatey with a yummy mint center.

Makes about 4 dozen

1 c. all-purpose flour
1 c. sugar
1 c. plus 6 T. butter, softened
　　and divided
4 eggs, beaten
16-oz. can chocolate syrup
2 c. powdered sugar
1 T. water
1/2 t. mint extract
3 drops green food coloring
1 c. semi-sweet chocolate chips

Beat flour, sugar, 1/2 cup butter, eggs and syrup in a large bowl until smooth; pour into a greased 13"x9" baking pan. Bake at 350 degrees for 25 to 30 minutes, or until top springs back when lightly touched. Cool completely in pan. Combine powdered sugar and 1/2 cup butter, water, mint extract and food coloring in a bowl; beat until smooth. Spread over brownies; chill. Melt chocolate chips and remaining butter in a double boiler; stir until smooth. Pour over chilled mint layer; cover and chill until set. Cut into small squares to serve.

Double Chocolate-Mint Brownies

Terri Lotz-Ganley, South Euclid, OH

Double-Dark Chocolate Brownies

If you love chocolate, you'll call this brownie your all-time favorite.

Makes 1-1/2 dozen

1-1/2 c. butter, melted
3 c. sugar
2 t. chocolate or vanilla extract
1 t. almond extract
6 eggs, beaten
1-1/2 c. all-purpose flour
1 c. baking cocoa
1-1/2 t. baking powder
1 t. salt
1 c. semi-sweet chocolate chips

Combine melted butter, sugar and extracts in a large bowl; stir well. Add eggs and beat well with spoon. Combine flour, cocoa, baking powder and salt in a separate bowl. Gradually add flour mixture to butter mixture, beating until well blended. Add chocolate chips and stir well. Spread batter evenly in a greased 13"x9" glass baking pan. Bake at 350 degrees for 30 to 40 minutes, until a toothpick inserted in center comes out clean. Cool completely in pan on a wire rack; cut into bars. Store in an airtight container.

Diana Pindell, Wooster, OH

Brown Sugar Brownies

These yummy blondies are so popular with the kids when they bring friends home after school.

Makes 1-1/2 dozen

2/3 c. butter, softened
2-1/4 c. brown sugar, packed
4 eggs
1 t. vanilla extract
2 c. all-purpose flour
2 t. baking powder
1 t. salt
12-oz. pkg. semi-sweet chocolate chips

Beat butter and brown sugar in a large bowl with an electric mixer at medium speed until light and fluffy. Beat in eggs, one at a time, just until blended. Beat in vanilla. Combine flour, baking powder and salt in a separate bowl; gradually add flour mixture to butter mixture, stirring until blended. Stir in chocolate chips; spoon batter into a greased 13"x9" baking pan. Bake at 350 degrees for 35 to 40 minutes, until a toothpick inserted in center comes out with a few moist crumbs. Cool completely in pan on a wire rack. Cut into squares. Store in an airtight container.

Brown Sugar Brownies

Laura Fuller, Fort Wayne, IN

Cookies & Cream Brownies

Pour yourself a frosty glass of milk and dig in!

Makes 2 dozen

1/2 c. baking cocoa
1/2 c. margarine, melted
1/2 c. brown sugar, packed
3/4 c. sugar, divided
3 eggs, divided
1/2 c. all-purpose flour
1 t. baking powder
1-1/2 t. vanilla extract, divided
12 chocolate sandwich cookies, crushed
8-oz. pkg. cream cheese, softened

In a large bowl, combine cocoa, margarine, brown sugar and 1/2 cup sugar; blend well. Add 2 eggs, one at a time, beating well after each addition. In a separate bowl, combine flour and baking powder; stir into cocoa mixture. Stir in one teaspoon vanilla and cookie crumbs. Spread into a greased 11"x7" baking pan. In another bowl, beat cream cheese and remaining sugar, egg and vanilla until smooth. Spoon cream cheese mixture over batter; cut through batter with a knife to swirl. Bake at 350 degrees for 25 to 30 minutes, until a toothpick inserted near the center comes out with moist crumbs. Cool completely. Cut into bars.

Mary Ann Clark, Indian Springs, OH

Birthday Brownies

My children have often requested these quick & easy brownies as treats for their birthdays.

Makes 1-1/2 to 2 dozen

3/4 c. butter, softened
1-1/4 c. sugar
1-1/4 c. brown sugar, packed
3 eggs, beaten
2-1/2 t. baking powder
1/2 t. salt
1 t. vanilla extract
2-1/4 c. all-purpose flour
12-oz. pkg. semi-sweet chocolate chips

Blend butter and sugars in a large bowl until very smooth. Add eggs, baking powder, salt and vanilla. Stir in flour; fold in chocolate chips. Spread in a greased 13"x9" baking pan. Bake at 400 degrees for 20 minutes, or until a toothpick inserted in the center comes out clean. Cut into squares.

COOKIE KNOW-HOW
For best results, start your cookie making with the ingredients at room temperature.

Birthday Brownies

Sherry Cecil, South Point, OH

Speedy Little Devils

When I was a child. this was my "special treat" that Mom made for me. Now that I have my own family, it has become one of my kids' favorite desserts and always takes me back to fond memories from my childhood!

Makes one dozen

18-1/4 oz. pkg. devil's food cake mix
1/2 c. butter, melted
1/2 c. creamy peanut butter
7-oz. jar marshmallow creme

In a large bowl, combine dry cake mix with melted butter; mix well. Reserve 1-1/2 cups of cake mixture for topping. Press remaining cake mixture into the bottom of an ungreased 13"x9" baking pan. In a separate bowl, blend peanut butter and marshmallow creme; gently spread over cake mixture. Sprinkle remaining cake mixture over top. Bake at 350 degrees for 20 minutes. Cool; cut into squares.

Dorothy Armijo, Dallas, TX

Chocolate-Butter Cream Squares

These scrumptious squares taste like a combination of brownies and buttercream candy...yum!

Makes 2 dozen

1/4 c. butter, softened
1/2 c. sugar
1 egg, beaten
1/2 c. all-purpose flour
1-oz. sq. unsweetened baking chocolate, melted
1/4 c. chopped nuts

Blend butter, sugar and egg in a bowl; stir in flour, chocolate and nuts. Spread evenly in a greased and floured 8"x8" baking pan. Bake at 350 degrees for 10 minutes. Cool; spread with Filling, then spread Icing over the top. Chill until set; cut into small squares.

Filling:
2 T. butter, softened
1 c. powdered sugar
1 T. whipping cream
1/2 t. vanilla extract

Blend all ingredients in a small bowl until smooth and creamy. Refrigerate 10 minutes before spreading.

Icing:
1-oz. sq. unsweetened baking chocolate
1 T. butter

Melt ingredients together in a double boiler over medium heat; stir until blended.

Chocolate-Butter Cream Squares

Sally Aken-Linke, Norfolk, NE

German Chocolate Cookie Bars

I like to use Mexican-blend vanilla extract for a richer flavor. Lightly frosting the bars while still warm seals in the moisture...so tasty!

Makes 1-1/2 dozen

1 egg, beaten
1/2 c. butter, melted and cooled
1/2 t. vanilla extract
18-1/2 oz. pkg. German chocolate
    cake mix
1 c. sweetened flaked coconut,
    divided
16-oz. container vanilla frosting

In a large bowl, beat egg, butter and vanilla; stir in dry cake mix and 1/2 cup coconut. Spray a 13"x9" baking pan with non-stick vegetable spray; spread batter in pan. Bake at 350 degrees for 25 to 30 minutes. Cool in pan for 10 minutes. Meanwhile, combine remaining coconut with frosting. Lightly spread 1/2 cup frosting over warm bars. Let cool completely; frost with remaining frosting. Cut into bars.

Jessica Parker, Mulvane, KS

Easy 4-Layer Marshmallow Brownies

Kids and adults love these colorful brownie bars! They are so much fun at parties and kids' birthdays!

Makes 2 dozen

18-1/2 oz. pkg. chocolate cake mix
1/4 c. butter, melted
1/4 c. water
3 c. mini marshmallows
1 c. candy-coated chocolates
1/2 c. chopped pecans

Combine dry cake mix, butter and water until blended; press into a greased 13"x9" baking pan. Bake at 375 degrees for 20 to 22 minutes. Layer marshmallows, chocolates and pecans over the top. Return to oven for an additional 3 to 5 minutes or until marshmallows melt; let cool. Cut into bars.

COOKIE KNOW-HOW
To cut perfect bars, score the pan of brownies first where they are to be cut, then cut all the way through with a sharp knife dipped in warm water.

Easy 4-Layer Marshmallow Brownies

Elizabeth Cisneros, Chino Hills, CA

The Best Blondies

For an extra-special dessert, serve each square topped with a scoop of ice cream and caramel sauce... delicious!

Makes one dozen

1 c. butter, melted
2 c. brown sugar, packed
2 eggs, beaten
2 t. vanilla extract
2 c. all-purpose flour
1/2 t. baking powder
1/4 t. salt
1 c. chopped pecans
1 c. white chocolate chips
3/4 c. toffee or caramel baking bits

Line a 13"x9" baking pan with parchment paper. Spray sides of pan with non-stick vegetable spray and set aside. In a large bowl, mix together butter and brown sugar. Beat in eggs and vanilla until mixture is smooth. Stir in flour, baking powder and salt; mix in pecans, chocolate chips and baking bits. Pour into prepared pan and spread evenly. Bake at 375 degrees for 30 to 40 minutes, until set in the middle. Allow to cool in pan before cutting into squares.

Sheila Gwaltney, Johnson City, TN

Quarterback Crunch Brownies

I made these one year for Christmas and my nephew Nick fell in love with them. Now every year he gets his very own pan full of them for his birthday on January 3rd!

Makes one dozen

1 c. butter, softened
2 c. sugar
4 eggs
6 T. baking cocoa
1 c. all-purpose flour
1-1/2 t. vanilla extract
1/2 t. salt
7-oz. jar marshmallow creme
2 c. crispy rice cereal
1 c. creamy peanut butter
12-oz. pkg. semi-sweet chocolate chips

Blend together butter and sugar in a large bowl. Add eggs, one at a time, beating after each addition. Stir in cocoa, flour, vanilla and salt. Spread batter into a greased 13"x9" baking pan. Bake at 350 degrees for 30 minutes. Let cool for 10 minutes. Spread with marshmallow creme and sprinkle with cereal, pressing lightly. In a saucepan over low heat, combine peanut butter and chocolate chips; stir until melted. Spread chocolate mixture over cereal. Let cool completely; cut into squares.

Quarterback Crunch Brownies

Barbara Girlardo, Pittsburgh, PA

Red Velvet Brownies

This is always a show-stopper brownie. If you don't want to make them as red, just use less food coloring.

Serves 16

4-oz. pkg. bittersweet chocolate
  baking bar, chopped
3/4 c. butter
2 c. sugar
4 eggs
1-1/2 c. all-purpose flour
1 T. red liquid food coloring
1-1/2 t. baking powder
1 t. vanilla extract
1/8 t. salt
Optional: chopped pecans

Line the bottom and sides of a 9"x9" baking pan with aluminum foil, allowing 2 to 4 inches to extend over sides; lightly grease foil. Microwave chocolate and butter in a large microwave-safe bowl about 2 minutes, until melted, stirring at 30-second intervals. Add sugar, whisking to blend. Add eggs, one at a time, whisking after each addition. Gently stir in flour and remaining

ingredients except pecans. Pour mixture into pan. Bake at 350 degrees for 40 minutes, until a toothpick inserted in center comes out clean. Cool completely in pan. Spread with Cream Cheese Frosting; cut into bars. Top with chopped pecans, if desired. Store in refrigerator.

Cream Cheese Frosting:
8-oz. pkg. cream cheese, softened
3 T. butter, softened
1-1/2 c. powdered sugar
1/8 t. salt
1 t. vanilla extract

Beat cream cheese and butter in a large bowl with an electric mixer at medium speed until creamy. Gradually add powdered sugar and salt, beating until blended. Stir in vanilla.

Kathy Grashoff, Fort Wayne, IN

Cake Mix Brownies

My sweet sister-in-law gave me this recipe more than 30 years ago. So simple and tasty!

Makes one dozen

18-1/2 oz. pkg. devil's food cake mix
1 egg, beaten
1/3 c. oil
1/3 c. water
Garnish: chocolate frosting,
  chopped walnuts

Stir together all ingredients except garnish to make a thick batter. Spread in a greased 13"x9" baking pan. Bake at 350 degrees for 20 to 25 minutes. Cool; cut into squares. Ice squares with frosting and sprinkle with walnuts.

Cake Mix Brownies

Alicia Allen, Lakeside, AZ

Triple-Layered Brownies

I make these cake-type brownies for any get-together. Everyone begs for the recipe! Be sure to use creamy frosting instead of the whipped style.

Makes 2 dozen

20-oz. pkg. brownie mix
3 eggs, beaten
1/4 c. water
1/2 c. oil
16-oz. container cream cheese
    frosting
1 c. creamy peanut butter
12-oz. pkg. milk chocolate chips
2-1/2 c. crispy rice cereal

In a large bowl, stir dry brownie mix, eggs, water and oil just until combined. Grease the bottom of a 13"x9" glass baking pan; pour in batter. Bake at 350 degrees for 27 to 30 minutes. Cool in pan. Spread frosting over cooled brownies; refrigerate until set. In a saucepan, melt peanut butter and chocolate chips together over low heat, stirring frequently until smooth. Remove from heat. Mix in cereal and spread evenly over frosting. Refrigerate until set. Cut into squares.

Nikki Matusiak, Zelienople, PA

Tiger's Eye Brownies

These are now our family's favorite brownies...delicious!

Makes 1-1/2 dozen

10-oz. pkg. peanut butter chips
1/2 c. butter
1-2/3 c. sugar
1-1/4 c. all-purpose flour
1/2 t. salt
1/2 t. baking powder
3 eggs, beaten
1 c. dark or semi-sweet chocolate
    chips

In a saucepan over low heat, melt peanut butter chips and butter together, stirring frequently, until smooth. Remove from heat. Stir in remaining ingredients in the order listed. Spread batter in an ungreased 13"x9" baking pan. Bake at 350 degrees for 25 to 30 minutes, until center is set. Cool; cut into squares.

Tiger's Eye Brownies

Flo Burtnett, Gage, OK

Fudge Brownie Pie

This recipe first appeared in a 1914 cookbook...it's as good now as it was then.

Serves 6

1 c. sugar
1/2 c. butter, melted
2 eggs, beaten
1/2 c. all-purpose flour
1/3 c. baking cocoa
1/4 t. salt
1 t. vanilla extract
1/2 c. chopped walnuts
Garnish: vanilla ice cream

Beat sugar and butter together. Add eggs; mix well. Stir in flour, cocoa and salt; mix in vanilla and nuts. Pour into a greased and floured 9" pie plate. Bake at 350 degrees for 25 to 30 minutes. Cut into wedges; top with ice cream.

Sandy Bernards, Valencia, CA

Divine Praline Brownies

These rich and thick brownies are super easy to make and impress everyone who takes a yummy bite!

Makes one dozen

22-1/2 oz. pkg. brownie mix
1/4 c. butter
1 c. brown sugar, packed
1 c. chopped pecans

Prepare brownie mix according to package directions. Spread batter in a greased 13"x9" baking pan. Set aside. Melt butter in a skillet over low heat; add brown sugar and pecans. Cook until sugar dissolves; drizzle over brownie batter. Bake at 350 degrees for 25 to 30 minutes. Cool and cut into bars. Keep refrigerated.

COOKIE KNOW-HOW
Nuts add texture and flavor to brownies. Try adding different nuts to the batter, such as walnuts, pecans and macadamia nuts to equal the amount listed.

Divine Praline Brownies

Vicki Nelson, Puyallup, WA

Mother's Zucchini Brownies

My mother gave me this recipe years ago after I married and started growing a garden. Like everyone else, I was always looking for ways to use up zucchini.

Makes one dozen

2 c. all-purpose flour
1 t. salt
1/3 c. baking cocoa
1-1/2 t. baking soda
1-1/4 c. sugar
1/2 c. oil
1 egg, beaten
2 c. zucchini, grated
Garnish: chocolate frosting or
    powdered sugar

In a bowl, stir together flour, salt, cocoa and baking soda. Mix in sugar, oil, egg and zucchini. Spread into a lightly greased 15"x10" jelly-roll pan. Bake at 350 degrees for 20 minutes. Let cool; garnish as desired.

Jo Ann, Gooseberry Patch

Chocolate Cappuccino Brownies

Chewy and chocolatey together, with a touch of coffee flavor...delicious!

Makes 1-1/2 to 2 dozen

1/2 c. butter, melted
1 c. brown sugar, packed
2 T. instant coffee granules
3 eggs, slightly beaten
1 t. vanilla extract
1/2 c. brewed coffee, cooled
1 t. baking powder
1/2 t. salt
1-1/4 c. all-purpose flour, sifted
1/3 c. plus 1 T. baking cocoa
1 c. chopped walnuts
1 c. semi-sweet chocolate chips
Garnish: powdered sugar

In a bowl, combine butter, brown sugar and coffee granules; blend well. Add eggs, vanilla and cooled coffee; stir. In a separate bowl, combine baking powder, salt, flour and cocoa; add to butter mixture. Stir in walnuts and chocolate chips, mixing well. Pour batter into a greased 13"x9" baking pan. Bake at 350 degrees for 25 to 30 minutes. Allow brownies to cool. Cut into squares. Dust with powdered sugar before serving.

Chocolate Cappuccino Brownies

Jen Stout, Blandon, PA

Swirled Peanut Butter Cheesecake Bars

This is a rich and delicious dessert for all cheesecake lovers!

Makes 1-1/2 dozen

2 c. graham cracker crumbs
1/2 c. butter, melted
1-1/3 c. sugar, divided
2 8-oz. pkgs. cream cheese, softened
1/4 c. all-purpose flour
12-oz. can evaporated milk
2 eggs, beaten
1 T. vanilla extract
6-oz. pkg. peanut butter & milk
    chocolate chips

Combine cracker crumbs, butter and 1/3 cup sugar. Press into the bottom of an ungreased 13"x9" baking pan. Beat cream cheese, remaining sugar and flour until smooth. Gradually beat in evaporated milk, eggs and vanilla.

Reserve one cup cream cheese mixture; spread remaining mixture over crust. Microwave peanut butter and chocolate chips in a microwave-safe bowl on medium for one to 2 minutes; stir until smooth. Stir in reserved cream cheese mixture; pour over bars. Swirl mixtures with a spoon, pulling plain cream cheese mixture up to the surface. Bake at 325 degrees for 40 to 45 minutes, until set. Cool in pan on a wire rack; refrigerate until firm. Cut into bars.

Judy Renkiewicz, Grand Marais, MN

Chocolate Coconut Brownies

These brownies are full of flavor and texture...yum!

Makes one dozen

3 c. all-purpose flour
2 c. sugar
6 T. baking cocoa
2 t. baking soda
1/2 t. salt
1/2 c. butter, melted
2 eggs, beaten
3 T. vinegar
1-1/2 c. water
1 c. flaked coconut
1 c. coarsely chopped pecans or
    walnuts

Mix together flour, sugar, cocoa, baking soda and salt in a large bowl. Add butter, eggs, vinegar and water. Mix well. Fold in coconut and nuts. Bake at 350 degrees for about 30 minutes, until a toothpick comes out clean. Cool and cut into squares.

Chocolate Coconut Brownies

Norwegian Kringla, p. 104

CHAPTER FOUR

Fancy & Specialty Cookies

Chocolate Waffle Sticks, p. 100

Stained Glass Cookies, p. 92

Tara Horton, Delaware, OH

Baklava Cookies

All the wonderful flavor of baklava without all the work!

Makes 2 dozen

1/4 c. butter, sliced
1/2 c. powdered sugar
3 T. honey
3/4 c. walnuts, finely chopped
1/4 t. cinnamon
1 t. lemon zest
18-oz. pkg. refrigerated sugar cookie
   dough

Melt butter in a saucepan over low heat; stir in powdered sugar and honey. Bring to a boil and remove from heat. Stir in walnuts, cinnamon and lemon zest. Let cool 30 minutes. Shape cooled butter mixture into 1/2-inch balls; set aside. Cut packaged cookie dough evenly into 12 slices; cut each slice in half. Roll each piece of dough into a ball; place on greased baking sheets, 2 inches apart. Bake at 350 degrees for 6 minutes. Remove cookies from oven; press a butter-mixture ball into the center of each cookie. Bake an additional 6 to 7 minutes, until edges are golden. Transfer to wire racks; cool completely.

Cathy Hillier, Salt Lake City, UT

Raspberry Linzer Tarts

These cookies are divine! Use any flavor of fruit preserves or jam that you enjoy.

Makes one dozen

1-1/4 c. butter, softened
2/3 c. sugar
1-1/2 c. almonds, ground
1/8 t. cinnamon
2 c. all-purpose flour
6 T. raspberry preserves, divided
Garnish: powdered sugar

In a bowl, blend butter and sugar until light and fluffy. Stir in almonds, cinnamon and flour, 1/2 cup at a time. Cover and refrigerate for about one hour. On a floured surface, roll out dough 1/8-inch thick. Cut out 24 circles with a 2-1/2 inch round cookie cutter. Cut out the centers of 12 circles with a 1/2-inch mini cookie cutter; leave the remaining 12 circles uncut. Arrange on parchment paper-lined baking sheets, one inch apart. Bake at 325 degrees for 10 to 12 minutes, until golden. Cool completely on wire racks. Thinly spread half of the preserves over uncut circles; top with cut-out cookies. Spoon remaining jam into cut-outs; sprinkle with powdered sugar.

Raspberry Linzer Tarts

Karin Anderson, Hillsboro, OH

German Apple Streusel Kuchen

These always disappear fast from our cookie tray!

Makes 2 dozen

16-oz. loaf frozen bread dough,
    thawed
4 Granny Smith apples, peeled,
    cored and thinly sliced
3/4 c. plus 1/3 c. sugar, divided
1 t. cinnamon
1 T. vanilla extract
1/4 c. sliced almonds
1-1/4 c. all-purpose flour
1/4 c. butter, melted

Let dough rise according to package directions. Spread dough in a greased 16"x11" baking sheet. Cover dough with plastic wrap and let rise in a warm place (85 degrees), free from drafts, 20 to 25 minutes, until double in size. Mix apples, 3/4 cup sugar, cinnamon and vanilla; spread apple mixture evenly over dough. Sprinkle with almonds. Combine flour, butter and remaining sugar in a separate bowl; mix until crumbly and spread evenly over apple layer. Bake at 375 degrees for 25 minutes, or until a toothpick inserted in center comes out clean. Cool completely in pan on a wire rack; cut into squares.

Shannon Sitko, Warren, OH

Grandmother's Waffle Cookies

My Grandmother Blanche always made these delicious cookies...we loved them then and we still do!

Makes 3 dozen

1 c. butter, melted and slightly
    cooled
4 eggs, beaten
1 c. sugar
1 c. brown sugar, packed
2 t. vanilla extract
4 c. all-purpose flour
Optional: frosting and sprinkles

Mix together melted butter, eggs and sugars; add vanilla. Slowly stir in flour. Drop batter by teaspoonfuls onto a preheated ungreased waffle iron. Check cookies after about one minute. Cookies are done when they are a medium golden in center and light golden at the edges. Dip in frosting and sprinkles if desired.

Grandmother's Waffle Cookies

Jennifer Peterson, Ankeny, IA

Stained Glass Cookies

These cookies are almost like magic! The sugar cookies are baked first and then the crushed candy is added and baked again. You can use whatever cookie cutters you like. Just be sure the cutters have a large enough area in the center to cut out a smaller shape such as a circle or square. For the Royal Icing recipe and tips and ideas for decorating these beautiful little gems, see pages 94-95.

Makes about 3 dozen

2/3 c. butter, softened
3/4 c. sugar
1 t. baking powder
1/4 t. teaspoon salt
1 egg, beaten
1 t. milk
1 t. vanilla extract
1/4 t. almond extract
2 c. all-purpose flour
Assorted clear hard candies,
   unwrapped

In a large bowl, combine butter, sugar, baking powder and salt. Beat with an electric mixer on medium-high speed until fluffy. Beat in egg until well combined. Beat in milk and extracts. Gradually add flour, beating on low speed, until combined. Wrap dough in parchment or wax paper and chill for one hour, or until no longer sticky and easy to roll out. On a lightly floured surface roll out dough to 1/8 to 1/4 inch thick. Use desired cookie cutters to cut out dough and place one inch apart on parchment paper-lined baking sheets. Use smaller cutters to cut out centers from cookie dough shapes. Bake at 375 degrees for 6 to 8 minutes or until cookies are done and edges are barely golden. Cool completely on a wire rack. Repeat with remaining dough.

To add the candy "stained glass," reduce the oven temperature to 300 degrees. To fill cookies with candy windows, place desired colors of hard candy in separate small plastic zipping storage bags. Coarsely crush candies in bags with a mallet. Arrange baked cookies on an aluminum foil-lined baking sheet. Use a spoon to fill the cut-outs of cookies with crushed candy. Bake for 3 to 5 minutes or just until candy is melted. Let cool completely on foil. When cool, peel cookies from the foil.

To decorate the cookies, thin some of the Royal Icing by adding a small amount of water to make icing a pourable consistency. Use a clean artist's brush to brush icing onto tops of cookies. Place the thick Royal Icing in a disposable decorating bag. Snip a very small opening from tip of bag. Pipe outlines onto iced cookies as desired. Let cookies dry several hours before storing or serving.

Continued on page 94

Stained Glass Cookies

Frosted Stained Glass Cookies

Royal Icing:
2 c. powdered sugar, sifted
4 t. meringue powder
1/2 t. cream of tartar
4 t. cold water

In a medium mixing bowl, combine powdered sugar, meringue powder and cream of tartar. Add cold water. Beat with electric mixer on low speed until combined; beat on medium-high speed for 5 to 8 minutes or until mixture is very thick and fluffy. Keep prepared icing covered with plastic wrap when not using. Use thick icing for piping. Thin as directed for icing. Makes about 2 cups.

Windowpane Cookies

Unfrosted Stained Glass Cookies

TIPS FOR MAKING STAINED GLASS COOKIES:

- Always be sure the hard candy is set before moving the cookie from the baking sheet.

- To make the inside of the cookies look more like stained glass, mix the colors of the crushed hard candies when adding to the open area.

- You can leave the outside cookies without frosting or use Royal Icing to decorate. Thin the icing and spread on the cookie. Then pipe little dots and outlines around the center section of the cookie with the thicker icing.

- To make the inside of a square cookie look like a magic and wintry windowpane, add a crisscross line of icing in the middle and then pipe tiny snowflakes on the solid candy area.

Lilia Keune, Biloxi, MS

Russian Tea Cookies

This is an amazing cookie that melts in your mouth. The recipe was given to me by my friend's grandma. It's my go-to recipe when I need something really delicious.

Makes 4 dozen

1-1/2 c. butter, softened
1 t. salt
3/4 c. powdered sugar
1 T. vanilla extract
3 c. all-purpose flour
2 c. mini semi-sweet chocolate chips
1/2 c. pecans, finely chopped
Optional: 1/4 c. powdered sugar

In a large bowl, beat together butter, salt, powdered sugar and vanilla. Gradually add flour and mix well. Stir in chocolate chips and pecans. Shape tablespoonfuls of dough into one-inch logs. Place on ungreased baking sheets. Bake at 375 degrees for 12 minutes, or until lightly golden. If desired, sift powdered sugar over hot cookies on baking sheets. Let stand for 10 minutes; remove cookies to wire racks. When cool, immediately store in an airtight container.

Elizabeth Blackstone, Racine, WI

Dad's Giant Cookie

What better way to celebrate a big-hearted dad than with a big, hearty cookie? Easily adapted for other special occasions too.

Serves 12

1 c. butter, softened
1-1/2 c. brown sugar, packed
1 t. vanilla extract
2 eggs, beaten
2-1/4 c. all-purpose flour
1 t. baking powder
1/2 t. salt
2 c. milk chocolate chips

In a large bowl, combine butter, brown sugar and vanilla. Beat with an electric mixer on medium speed for 5 minutes. Add eggs, one at a time, beating well after each; set aside. In a small bowl, combine flour, baking powder and salt; mix well. Gradually beat flour mixture into butter mixture; stir in chocolate chips. Spread batter on a parchment paper-lined 14" round pizza pan. Bake at 375 degrees for 30 to 40 minutes, until golden. Cool in pan for 10 minutes. Carefully transfer to a serving platter; cool completely. To serve, cut into wedges.

Dad's Giant Cookie

Jennifer Peterson, Ankeny, IA

French Macaroons

These classic cookies always bring rave reviews. Absolutely beautiful!

Makes 3 dozen

1-3/4 c. powdered sugar, sifted
1 c. almond flour, sifted
3 egg whites, room temperature
1/2 t. vanilla extract
1/4 t. cream of tartar
1/8 t. salt
1/4 c. superfine or granulated sugar
few drops desired food coloring

Line 2 baking sheets with parchment paper. Trace 1-1/2 inch round circles onto parchment sheets using a pencil and a small measuring cup or other round shape as a guide. You should have about 35 circles per cookie sheet. Flip parchment sheets over so pencil marks are underneath but are still visible; set aside. In a medium bowl, whisk together powdered sugar and almond flour; set aside. Place egg whites, vanilla and cream of tartar in a large bowl. Beat with an electric mixer on medium-high speed until frothy. Gradually add superfine sugar and continue beating until stiff peaks form, scraping sides of bowl as needed. Beat in desired food coloring. Gently fold in almond flour mixture, adding 1/3 at a time, until well combined. Place dough in a disposable decorating bag. Cut a 1/2-inch opening from tip of bag. Pipe uniform circles of batter onto prepared baking sheets. Pop any bubbles in batter with a toothpick. Let stand for 15 to 30 minutes or until tops look dry. Bake at 325 degrees, one baking sheet at a time, for about 10 to 12 minutes or until sides look dry. Let cool on baking sheets. Peel macaroons from parchment paper when completely cooled. Sandwich 2 cookies together with a layer of piped Vanilla Filling between.

Vanilla Filling:
1/4 c. butter, softened
2 oz. cream cheese, softened
2 c. powdered sugar, divided
1 t. vanilla extract
2 t. milk

In a medium bowl, beat together butter and cream cheese. Gradually add one cup powdered sugar. Add vanilla extract and milk. Gradually beat in remaining powdered sugar. Place filling in a disposable decorating bag fitted with a medium star tip.

French Macaroons

Jeanette Toscano, Pomona, NY

Mom's Italian Cookies

When my parents emigrated to the U.S. in the 1960s, they brought this recipe with them. We have made them for years and love them!

Makes 3 dozen

5-1/2 c. all-purpose flour
1 T. plus 2 t. baking powder
3/4 c. butter, softened
1-1/2 c. sugar
6 eggs, beaten
zest of 2 lemons
juice of 2 lemons
3-1/2 c. powdered sugar
Optional: candy sprinkles

In a large bowl, mix together flour, baking powder, butter and sugar; form a well in the center. Add eggs and lemon zest; knead until dough is smooth. Form into 2-inch balls. Roll each ball on a floured surface into a 7-inch rope. Twist ropes into knots; place on lightly greased baking sheets. Bake at 350 degrees for 15 to 18 minutes. Cool on a wire rack. Combine lemon juice and powdered sugar; drizzle over cookies. Decorate with sprinkles, if desired.

Judy Bailey, Des Moines, IA

Chocolate Waffle Sticks

You will need a waffle-stick waffle iron for these little goodies if you want to have the perfect little stick. Or, you can also use your regular waffle iron and cut the cooked waffle into sticks before dipping into the chocolate. Either way, it is yummy!

Makes 10 to 15 waffle sticks

1-1/4 c. all-purpose flour
1 t. baking powder
1/2 t. salt
1 c. sugar
1/2 c. baking cocoa
2 eggs, lightly beaten
1 c. buttermilk
2 t. vanilla extract
4 T. butter, melted
Garnish: melted chocolate chips,
    assorted jimmies

Preheat waffle maker. In a medium bowl, combine flour, baking powder, salt, sugar and cocoa. Add eggs, buttermilk and vanilla and whisk until consistent. Gradually add melted butter, whisking until smooth. Using a measuring cup, fill cooking reservoirs with batter. Close waffle iron; bake for about 3 to 6 minutes, to desired doneness. Cool slightly. Dip sticks into melted chocolate. Sprinkle with jimmies.

Chocolate Waffle Sticks

Lisa Johnson, Hallsville, TX

Almond Cream Spritz

These little German cookies are rich, buttery and very pretty. Leave them plain or add a few almonds on top.

Makes 5 dozen

1 c. butter, softened
3-oz. pkg. cream cheese, softened
1/2 c. sugar
1/2 t. almond extract
1/4 t. vanilla extract
2 c. all-purpose flour
Optional: 1/2 c. almonds, finely chopped

Beat butter and cream cheese in a large bowl with an electric mixer at medium speed until well blended. Add sugar and extracts; beat well. Stir in flour. Cover and chill dough 30 minutes, or until easy to handle. Place dough in a cookie press and press out cookies onto ungreased baking sheets; sprinkle with almonds if desired. Bake at 375 degrees for 8 to 10 minutes, until edges are lightly golden; remove to wire racks to cool. Store in an airtight container.

Lisa Ashton, Aston, PA

Swedish Ginger Cookies

The orange zest really brings out the flavor of the ginger.

Makes about 8 dozen

1 c. butter, softened
1-1/2 c. sugar
1 egg, beaten
2 T. dark corn syrup
1 T. water
1-1/2 T. orange zest
3-1/4 c. all-purpose flour
2 t. baking soda
2 t. cinnamon
1 t. ground ginger
Garnish: sugar

Beat together butter and sugar in a large bowl; add egg and beat until light and fluffy. Add corn syrup, water and zest; stir well and set aside. In a separate bowl, mix together flour, baking soda and spices. Gradually add flour mixture to butter mixture. Roll dough into walnut-size balls; place on ungreased baking sheets. Flatten cookies gently with a fork dipped in sugar. Bake at 375 degrees for 8 to 10 minutes. Remove to wire racks to cool.

Swedish Ginger Cookies

Miriam Schultz, Waukee, IA

Norwegian Kringla

There are many variations of this classic Scandinavian cookie that varies from region to region. They are usually served without frosting, but a little frosting dresses them up for special parties.

Makes 4 dozen

4-1/2 c. all-purpose flour
1 t. baking soda
1 c. sour cream
1 egg
1-3/4 c. sugar
1/2 c. milk
2 T. butter, melted
1 t. vanilla
Optional: candy sprinkles

In a bow,l whisk together flour and baking soda; set aside. In a large bowl beat together sour cream, egg and sugar. Beat with an electric mixer on medium speed until well combined. Beat in milk, melted butter and vanilla. Gradually add flour mixture, beating on low speed, until combined. Remove dough from bowl and wrap in plastic wrap. Chill several hours or overnight, until firm. On a lightly floured surface, shape dough into balls, 2 tablespoons per ball. With hands, roll balls on lightly floured surface into long ropes about 12 inches long. On parchment paper-lined baking sheets, shape ropes into pretzels by making a loop, twisting ends twice, then folding ends over to other side of loop. Leave at least 2 inches of space between kringla on baking sheet. Bake for 6 minutes. With baking sheet in oven, turn broiler on. Broil for one minute or just until kringla are done and edges have a hint of browning. Watch closely to prevent overbrowning. Remove baking sheet from oven; return setting to bake at 400 degrees. Transfer kringla to a wire rack to cool. Repeat with remaining dough. If desired, spread Powdered Sugar Icing over cooled tops of kringla and top with sprinkles.

Powdered Sugar Icing:
2 c. powdered sugar
2 T. milk
1/2 t. vanilla extract

In a medium bowl combine powdered sugar, milk and vanilla. Whisk until smooth, adding more powdered sugar or milk as needed to make icing desired consistency.

Norwegian Kringla

Cheryl Bastian, Northumberland, PA

Sour Cream Drop Cookies

These rich cookies are one of our family favorites. They seem very European when served with a spot of tea.

Makes 3 dozen

3/4 c. butter, softened
1-1/2 c. sugar
2 eggs, beaten
1 t. vanilla extract
1/2 t. lemon or orange extract
8-oz. container sour cream
3 c. all-purpose flour
1 t. baking powder
1 t. baking soda

Beat butter and sugar in a large bowl with an electric mixer at medium speed until fluffy. Add eggs, vanilla and lemon or orange extract; mix well. Fold in sour cream; set aside. Combine remaining ingredients in a separate bowl; gradually add to butter mixture. Drop by teaspoonfuls onto greased baking sheets. Bake at 350 degrees for 10 to 12 minutes. Remove to wire racks and cool completely. Store in an airtight container.

Sandy Bootham, Camden, MI

Italian Cheese Cookies

A co-worker gave me this recipe years ago...it has become one of my husband's favorites!

Makes about 4 dozen

1 c. butter, softened
2 c. sugar
1 t. vanilla extract
1 t. salt
15-oz. container ricotta cheese
4 c. all-purpose flour
1 t. baking soda

In a large bowl, combine butter, sugar, vanilla, salt and ricotta cheese. Beat with an electric mixer on medium speed until blended. Gradually stir in flour, then baking soda. Drop dough by teaspoonfuls onto ungreased baking sheets. Bake at 350 degrees for 10 to 13 minutes. Cool on wire racks. Frost cooled cookies with Sweet Vanilla Icing.

Sweet Vanilla Icing:
2/3 c. plus 1 T. sweetened condensed milk
1/2 c. butter, softened
1 t. vanilla extract
2 c. powdered sugar
Optional: few drops red food coloring

Combine all ingredients except food coloring in a bowl; beat with electric mixer on medium speed until smooth. Stir in food coloring, if using.

Italian Cheese Cookies

Kimberly Pfleiderer, Galion, OH

Mexican Tea Cookies

Dusted in powdered sugar...these cookies are heavenly.

Makes about 3-1/2 dozen

1 c. butter, softened
1/4 c. powdered sugar
2 t. vanilla extract
1 T. water
2 c. all-purpose flour
1 c. chopped pecans
Garnish: powdered sugar

With an electric mixer on medium speed, blend together butter and powdered sugar; add vanilla, water and flour. Stir in pecans. Shape dough in one-inch balls. Arrange on an ungreased baking sheet. Bake at 300 degrees for 20 minutes. Remove from oven. When cool, roll in powdered sugar.

Ardith Field, Goldfield, IA

Raspberry-Almond Bars

Almond paste makes everything rich and delicious! This recipe reminds us of the Dutch letter pastries that we love to buy in a Dutch community near us.

Makes 2 dozen

1 c. butter, softened
8-oz. pkg. almond paste
2 eggs, beaten
2 c. sugar
2 c. all-purpose flour
1/2 c. raspberry jam, melted
1/2 c. sliced almonds

Line a 13"x9" baking pan with foil, extending foil over edges. Coat foil with non-stick vegetable spray; set aside. In a large bowl, beat butter, almond paste and eggs with an electric mixer on medium speed until combined. Add sugar; beat until light and fluffy. Gradually beat in flour on low speed until combined. Spread batter in prepared baking pan. Drizzle top with melted jam. Using a table knife or thin metal spatula, swirl jam into the dough. Sprinkle with almonds. Bake at 350 degrees for 35 to 40 minutes or until top is golden brown. Cool in pan on a wire rack. Use foil to lift out uncut bars. Cut into bars.

Raspberry-Almond Bars

Tessa Floehr, Marysville, OH

Raspberry-Marshmallow Cookie Pizza

A scrumptious dessert pizza...fancy enough to serve at a holiday tea, yet simple enough for kids' parties too.

Makes 20 to 24 servings

18-oz. tube refrigerated sugar cookie
   dough
7-oz. jar marshmallow creme
12-oz. jar seedless raspberry jam
1 c. milk chocolate chips

Spray a 12" pizza pan with non-stick vegetable spray. Spread out dough evenly in the pan, using your fingers to flatten. Pinch up dough to form a rim around the edges. Bake at 350 degrees for 12 to 18 minutes, until golden. Let cool completely on pan. When cooled, spread marshmallow creme evenly over cookie to within 1/2-inch of edge. Spread jam over marshmallow creme; set aside. Place chocolate chips in a microwave-safe bowl. Microwave on high for one minute; stir. Microwave an additional 10 to 20 seconds, stirring until smooth and melted. Drizzle melted chocolate over cookie. Chill for at least one hour. To serve, cut into thin wedges

Jo Ann, Gooseberry Patch

Crunchy Biscotti

In the afternoon or after dinner, you'll crave these treats with your next cup of coffee.

Makes about 3 dozen

1/4 c. oil
2 eggs, beaten
2 egg whites, beaten
1-1/4 c. sugar
3-1/3 c. all-purpose flour
2-1/2 t. baking powder
1/2 t. salt
Optional: melted white chocolate

In a large bowl, whisk together oil, eggs, egg whites and sugar; set aside. Mix flour, baking powder and salt in a separate bowl. Blend flour mixture into oil mixture. Divide dough into 3 portions; knead each portion 5 to 6 times and shape into a ball. Shape each ball into a 9-inch log; flatten slightly. Place on a parchment paper-lined 17"x11" jelly-roll sheet. Bake at 375 degrees for 25 minutes. Remove from oven; place logs on a cutting board. With a serrated bread knife, slice logs 1/2-inch thick on a slight diagonal. Return slices to baking sheet, cut-side up. Bake at 375 degrees for an additional 10 minutes. Turn over; continue baking for 5 to 7 minutes. Let cool; drizzle with white chocolate, if desired. Store in an airtight container.

Crunchy Biscotti

Lemon-Macadamia Cookies, p. 148

CHAPTER FIVE

Favorite Drop Cookies

Double Chocolate Cookies, p. 122   **Mom's Monster Cookies, p. 118**

Regina Vining, Warwick, RI

Cool Mint Chocolate Swirls

Chocolatey cookies topped with a cool, refreshing mint wafer.

Makes 3 dozen

3/4 c. butter
1-1/2 c. brown sugar, packed
2 T. water
12-oz. pkg. semi-sweet chocolate
　chips
2 eggs, beaten
2-1/2 c. all-purpose flour
1-1/4 t. baking soda
1/2 t. salt
2　4.67-oz. pkgs. crème de menthe
　thins

Combine butter, brown sugar and water in a large saucepan. Cook, stirring occasionally over medium heat until butter melts and mixture is smooth. Remove from heat. Add chocolate chips, stirring until melted; cool 10 minutes. Pour chocolate mixture into a large bowl; add eggs, one at a time, stirring until well blended. Combine flour, baking soda and salt in a separate bowl, stirring to mix; add flour mixture to chocolate mixture, stirring well. Cover and chill one hour. Use a cookie scoop to drop batter 2 inches apart on greased baking sheets. Bake at 350 degrees for 8 to 10 minutes, being careful not to overbake. Press one crème de menthe candy onto each warm cookie and let stand one minute; use back of a spoon to swirl softened candy over each cookie. Remove to wire racks to cool completely.

Vickie, Gooseberry Patch

Soft Pumpkin Cookies

My family prefers a soft cookie and these are their favorite ones!

Makes 2-1/2 dozen

2-1/2 c. all-purpose flour
1 t. baking powder
1 t. baking soda
1-1/2 t. cinnamon
1-1/2 c. sugar
1/2 c. butter, softened
1 c. canned pumpkin
1 egg, beaten
1 t. vanilla extract

Combine flour, baking powder, baking soda and cinnamon in a bowl. Beat together sugar and butter in a separate bowl until blended. Stir in pumpkin, egg and vanilla until smooth. Gradually add flour and sugar mixtures and stir well. Drop by rounded tablespoonfuls onto greased baking sheets. Bake at 350 degrees for 15 to 18 minutes, or until edges are firm. Cool on baking sheets for 2 minutes, then transfer to a wire rack. Cool completely; drizzle Glaze over cookies.

Glaze:
1 c. powdered sugar
2 T. milk
1 t. butter, melted
1 t. vanilla extract

Combine ingredients in a small bowl; mix until smooth.

Soft Pumpkin Cookies

Regina Vining, Warwick, RI

Lacy Florentine Cookies

Sweet and buttery...just like my Italian grandmother used to make.

Makes 4 dozen

3/4 c. quick-cooking oats, uncooked
3/4 c. all-purpose flour
3/4 c. sugar
1/2 t. baking soda
1/2 t. salt
1 t. cinnamon
1-1/2 c. sliced almonds
1/2 c. plus 2 T. butter, melted
1/4 c. half-and-half
1/4 c. light corn syrup
1 t. vanilla extract
4 1-oz. sqs. semi-sweet baking
    chocolate, melted

Combine oats, flour, sugar, baking soda, salt and cinnamon in a large bowl; mix well. Add almonds and stir well. Add butter, half-and-half, corn syrup and vanilla; stir until well blended. Drop dough by tablespoonfuls onto aluminum foil-lined, greased baking sheets, 6 cookies per sheet, 3 inches apart. Bake, one pan at a time on the center rack, at 350 degrees for 7 to 9 minutes, until edges are golden. Cool on pans for 5 minutes; remove to wire racks to cool completely. Drizzle melted chocolate over cooled cookies. Store in an airtight container.

Rhonda Reeder, Ellicott City, MD

Mix-and-Go Chocolate Cookies

Just as decadent made with peanut butter or milk chocolate chips!

Makes about 2 dozen

15-1/2 oz. pkg. chocolate cake mix
1/2 c. butter, softened
2 eggs, beaten
1 c. white chocolate chips

In a bowl, combine dry cake mix, butter and eggs until smooth. Mix in chocolate chips. Drop by tablespoonfuls onto ungreased baking sheets. Bake at 350 degrees for 8 to 10 minutes. Let cool on baking sheet for 5 minutes; remove to wire rack to cool completely.

Mix-and-Go Chocolate Cookies

Lori Ritchey, Denver, PA

Blueberry Drop Cookies

As these cookies bake, the kitchen fills with a wonderful blueberry aroma. Serve them still warm, with a cold glass of milk...perfect!

Makes 5 dozen

3/4 c. butter, softened
1 c. sugar
1-1/2 t. lemon zest
2 eggs
2 c. all-purpose flour
2 t. baking powder
1/4 t. salt
Optional: cinnamon to taste
1/2 c. milk
1 c. blueberries

In a large bowl, blend together butter, sugar and zest. Add eggs, one at a time, beating well. In a separate bowl, combine flour, baking powder, salt and cinnamon, if desired. Add flour mixture to butter mixture alternately with milk, beating until smooth. Fold in blueberries. Drop by teaspoonfuls onto greased baking sheets. Bake at 375 degrees for 10 to 12 minutes. Cool on wire racks.

Susie Backus, Delaware, OH

Mom's Monster Cookies

Packed with lots of yummy favorites! But are they called "monster" because they're monstrously good, or because this makes a monstrous amount of cookies?

Makes 8 dozen large cookies

6 eggs, beaten
1 c. butter, softened
16-oz. pkg. brown sugar
2 c. sugar
2 T.. vanilla extract
6 T. corn syrup
1-1/2 c. creamy peanut butter
1-1/2 c. almond butter
4 t. baking soda
9 c. quick-cooking oats, uncooked
1-1/2 c. dark chocolate chips
1-1/2 c. cashews
1-1/2 c. candy-coated chocolates

In a very large bowl, mix all ingredients in the order listed. Drop dough by heaping tablespoonfuls onto ungreased cookie sheets. Flatten out slightly. Bake at 350 degrees for 12 to 16 minutes. Cool on wire racks.

Mom's Monster Cookies

Rebecca Kelly, Marion, IN

Mincemeat Cookies

These cookies will go fast! They're especially delicious warm, right out of the oven.

Makes about 6-1/2 dozen

1 c. shortening
1-1/2 c. sugar
3 eggs, beaten
3 c. all-purpose flour
1 t. baking soda
1/2 t. salt
9-oz. pkg. condensed mincemeat, crumbled
Optional: vanilla frosting

In a large bowl, beat shortening and sugar until fluffy. Add eggs; beat well and set aside. In a separate bowl, mix flour, baking soda and salt. Gradually add flour mixture to shortening mixture. Mix well; stir in mincemeat. Drop by rounded teaspoonfuls, 2 inches apart, onto greased baking sheets. Bake at 375 degrees for 8 to 10 minutes, until lightly golden. Cool; frost if desired.

Sharon Levandowski, Hoosick Falls, NY

Gram's Zucchini Cookies

Who would think zucchini could make these cookies so yummy?

Makes 4 dozen

3/4 c. butter, softened
1-1/2 c. sugar
1 egg, beaten
1 t. vanilla extract
1-1/2 c. zucchini, grated
2-1/2 c. all-purpose flour
2 t. baking powder
1 t. cinnamon
1/2 t. salt
1 c. chopped walnuts or almonds
6-oz. pkg. semi-sweet chocolate chips

Blend together butter and sugar in a bowl; beat in egg and vanilla. Stir in zucchini. In a separate bowl, combine flour, baking powder, cinnamon and salt; gradually add to butter mixture. Stir in nuts and chocolate chips. Drop by heaping teaspoonfuls onto greased baking sheets. Bake at 350 degrees for 13 to 15 minutes, until golden. Remove to wire racks to cool.

Gram's Zucchini Cookies

Kristi Watson, Highland Ranch, CO

Double Chocolate Cookies

Doubly delectable! For variety, use white chocolate chips.

Makes 3 dozen

1 c. butter, softened
1 c. sugar
1 c. brown sugar, packed
2 eggs, beaten
2 c. all-purpose flour
1/2 c. baking cocoa
1 t. baking soda
1 t. cream of tartar
1/2 t. salt
1 c. semi-sweet chocolate chips
Garnish: additional sugar

In a large bowl, mix butter, sugars and eggs; set aside. In another bowl, whisk together remaining ingredients except chocolate chips and garnish. Add flour mixture to butter mixture; stir until well blended. Stir in chocolate chips. Drop by teaspoonfuls onto ungreased baking sheets and sprinkle with sugar. Bake at 350 degrees for 8 to 10 minutes. Cool on a wire rack.

Norma Longnecker, Lawrenceville, IL

Pineapple Nut Cookies

I've enjoyed these cookies for years. I began making them when my children were small, and now I make them for my grandkids.

Makes about 3-1/2 dozen

1/2 c. butter, softened
1/3 c. brown sugar, packed
1 egg, beaten
2-1/2 c. all-purpose flour
1 t. baking soda
1/2 c. pecans, chopped
8-oz. can crushed pineapple in juice, drained
1/2 t. vanilla extract
Optional: thin frosting

Beat butter and sugar until light and fluffy; blend in egg. Combine flour and baking soda. Add to butter mixture; blend well. Stir in pecans, pineapple and vanilla; drop by teaspoonfuls onto ungreased baking sheets. Bake at 375 degrees for 10 to 12 minutes. Cool on wire racks. Drizzle with thin frosting if desired.

Pineapple Nut Cookies

Bunny Palmertree, Carrollton, MS

White Chocolate Cookies

This cookie recipe is the one my husband requests each Christmas. The white chocolate in these cookies makes them so pretty and yummy!

Makes 5 dozen

1 c. butter, softened
3/4 c. brown sugar, packed
1/2 c. sugar
1 egg, beaten
1/2 t. almond extract
2 c. all-purpose flour
1 t. baking soda
1/4 t. cinnamon
1/4 t. ground ginger
1/4 t. salt
6-oz. pkg. white baking chocolate, chopped
1-1/2 c. chopped pecans

Beat butter and sugars in a large bowl with an electric mixer at medium speed until smooth. Add egg and extract; beat well. Combine flour, baking soda, cinnamon, ginger and salt in a separate bowl, stirring to mix; add flour mixture to butter mixture, stirring well. Blend in chocolate and pecans. Drop by teaspoonfuls 2 inches apart onto greased baking sheets. Bake at 350 degrees for 10 to 12 minutes, until lightly golden. Remove to wire racks to cool. Store in an airtight container.

Peggy Cummings, Cibolo, TX

Simple Meringues

These beautiful white-as-snow meringues are a sweet dessert that everyone loves.

Makes 3 dozen

2 egg whites
1/8 t. cream of tartar
1/8 t. salt
3/4 c. sugar
1/2 t. vanilla extract

Beat egg whites in a large bowl with an electric mixer at high speed until foamy. Add cream of tartar and salt, beating until mixed; gradually add sugar, one tablespoon at a time, beating well after each addition until stiff peaks form. Stir in vanilla. Drop by teaspoonfuls 1-1/2 inches apart onto greased baking sheets. Bake at 250 degrees for 40 minutes, or until dry. Remove to wire racks to cool completely. Store in an airtight container.

COOKIE KNOW-HOW
When beating egg whites, be sure that the mixer beaters and bowl are clean and free of any fat. Even the tiniest bit of fat can keep your egg whites from beating up as they should.

Simple Meringues

Nancy Hannon, Lewistown, PA

Brown Sugar-Apple Cookies

Perfect for sharing with friends over a steamy pot of spiced tea.

Makes 3-1/2 to 4 dozen

1 c. brown sugar, packed
2 eggs, beaten
1/2 t. baking soda
1 t. cinnamon
1/2 t. salt
1/2 c. shortening
2 t. vanilla extract
2 c. all-purpose flour
1 c. Granny Smith or Gala apples,
    peeled, cored and sliced

In a large bowl, mix all ingredients together, stirring in apples last. Drop dough by teaspoonfuls onto ungreased baking sheets. Bake at 350 degrees for 8 to 10 minutes. Cool on wire racks.

COOKIE KNOW-HOW
If you want cookies to be all the same size, use a cookie scoop to measure each one as you put them on the cookie sheet.

Tracey Ten Eyck, Austin, TX

Chocolate Chip-Oat Cookies

This recipe was handed down to me by my mother, who lived well into her nineties. She made the best cookies ever!

Makes 4 dozen

1 c. butter
3/4 c. brown sugar, packed
3/4 c. sugar
2 eggs
1 t. hot water
1-1/2 c. all-purpose flour
1 t. baking soda
1 t. salt
12-oz. pkg. mini semi-sweet
    chocolate chips
2 c. long-cooking oats, uncooked
Optional: 1 c. nuts, finely chopped
1 t. vanilla extract

In a large bowl, beat butter until soft. Gradually add sugars, blending until light and fluffy. Add eggs, one at a time, beating well after each addition. Stir in hot water. In a separate bowl, mix together flour, baking soda and salt; gradually add flour mixture to butter mixture. Stir in chocolate chips, oats and nuts, if desired; mix thoroughly. Add vanilla and blend well. Drop by teaspoonfuls onto greased baking sheets. Bake at 350 degrees for 8 to 12 minutes, until golden. Remove to wire racks to cool.

Chocolate Chip-Oat Cookies

Vickie, Gooseberry Patch

Snowcap Cookies

Serve these with hot cocoa to help chase away the chills.

Makes 3 to 4 dozen

3/4 c. butter, softened
1 c. sugar
3 eggs
1 t. vanilla extract
6 1-oz. sqs. white baking chocolate, melted and cooled
3-1/2 c. all-purpose flour
1 t. baking powder
1 t. salt
1/8 t. nutmeg
1-1/2 c. chopped walnuts, toasted
Garnish: powdered sugar

Beat butter and sugar in a large bowl with an electric mixer at medium speed until light and fluffy. Add eggs, one at a time, beating until blended after each addition. Stir in vanilla; add melted chocolate, beating 30 seconds. Combine flour, baking powder, salt and nutmeg in a separate bowl, stirring to mix. Gradually add flour mixture to butter mixture, beating until blended. Fold in walnuts. Drop by tablespoonfuls onto greased baking sheets. Bake at 350 degrees for 10 to 12 minutes; remove to wire racks to cool completely. Garnish tops with powdered sugar. Store in an airtight container.

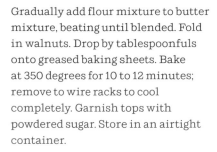

Myra Mitten, Goldfield, IA

Grandma Mitten's Oatmeal Cookies

These oatmeal cookies are full of flavor and disappear quickly!

Makes 3 dozen

1 c. butter, softened
1 c. sugar
2 eggs, beaten
1 t. baking soda
2 T. hot water
2 c. all-purpose flour
2-1/2 c. rolled oats, uncooked
1/2 t. salt
1 t. cinnamon
1/2 t. ground cloves
1 c. raisins
Optional: 1/4 c. chopped walnuts

In a bowl, blend butter and sugar until fluffy. Add eggs and mix well. Dissolve baking soda in hot water. Add to butter mixture and mix well; set aside. In a separate large bowl, mix flour, oats, salt and spices. Add to butter mixture and mix well. Stir in raisins and nuts, if using. Drop by tablespoonfuls onto lightly greased or parchment paper-lined baking sheets. Bake at 350 degrees for about 8 to 10 minutes, until lightly golden.

Grandma Mitten's Oatmeal Cookies

Jo Ann, Gooseberry Patch

Cherry Macaroons

If you like coconut macaroons, you'll love these! So easy to make, so irresistible to eat.

Makes 3-1/2 to 4 dozen

1 c. shortening
1 c. sugar
3 eggs
1/2 c. sour cream
3 c. all-purpose flour
1 t. baking powder
1/2 t. baking soda
1/2 t. salt
1 c. shredded coconut
1 t. lemon zest
1-1/2 t. almond extract
2/3 c. candied cherries

Combine shortening, sugar and eggs in a large bowl; mix well and stir in sour cream. Combine flour, baking powder, baking soda and salt in a separate bowl; mix well and add to shortening mixture. Fold in coconut, lemon zest and almond extract. Drop by tablespoonfuls onto ungreased baking sheets. Press one candied cherry onto center of each cookie. Bake at 400 degrees for 10 to 12 minutes. Remove from baking sheets; cool on wire racks.

Jennifer Holt, Fort Worth, TX

German Chocolate Delights

These cookies are quick to make because you use a cake mix as the dry ingredients for the batter. Adding all the other goodies just makes them yummy!

Makes about 4-1/2 dozen

18-1/4 oz. pkg. German chocolate cake mix
1/2 c. oil
2 eggs, beaten
1 single refrigerated chocolate pudding cup
1 c. semi-sweet chocolate chips
1/2 c. long-cooking oats, uncooked
1/2 c. chopped pecans
1 c. flaked coconut

Combine dry cake mix and remaining ingredients; blend well. Drop dough by rounded teaspoonfuls, 2 inches apart onto ungreased baking sheets. Bake at 350 degrees for 8 to 10 minutes, until set. Cool one minute before removing from baking sheets.

German Chocolate Delights

Nichole Sullivan, Santa Fe, TX

Grandma's Pecan Balls

These are a flavorful and moist, but not-too-sweet, cookie.

Makes about 3 dozen

1/4 c. butter, softened
8-oz. pkg. cream cheese, softened
1 egg yolk, beaten
1/2 t. vanilla extract
18-1/4 oz. pkg. butter pecan
   cake mix

With an electric mixer on medium speed, blend together butter and cream cheese. Add egg yolk and vanilla; blend thoroughly. Gradually beat in dry cake mix. Dough will be slightly stiff. Cover and refrigerate for 20 minutes. Drop dough by rounded teaspoonfuls onto greased or parchment paper-lined baking sheets. Bake at 350 degrees for 14 minutes or until lightly golden.

Mary Warren, Auburn, MI

Favorite Chocolate Chippers

The instant pudding in this cookie makes it extra chewy and good! We like pecans in this cookie, but walnuts work very well too.

Makes 3 dozen

3/4 c. butter, softened
3/4 c. brown sugar, packed
1/2 c. sugar
2 eggs, beaten
1 t. vanilla extract
3.4-oz. pkg. instant vanilla pudding
   mix
2 c. all-purpose flour
1 c. quick-cooking oats, uncooked
1 t. baking soda
12-oz. pkg. semi-sweet chocolate
   chips
1/4 c. chopped pecans
Optional: pecan halves

In a large bowl, beat together butter and sugars. Beat in eggs and vanilla. Add dry pudding mix, flour, oats and baking soda; mix just until well blended. Fold in chocolate chips and nuts. Drop by tablespoonfuls onto greased baking sheets. Top with pecan half if desired. Bake at 350 degrees for 12 to 14 minutes.

Favorite Chocolate Chippers

Paula Purcell, Plymouth Meeting, PA

Iced Carrot Cookies

One of my daughter's favorite stories was about a bunny who loved cakes and cookies made with carrots. Erin wanted to make these cookies whenever we read the story!

Makes 3 dozen

1 c. butter, softened
3/4 c. sugar
1 egg, beaten
1 c. carrot, peeled, cooked and
    mashed
2 c. all-purpose flour
2 t. baking powder
1/2 t. salt
1 t. vanilla extract
3 to 4 drops almond extract

In a large bowl, blend together butter and sugar; stir in egg and carrots. In a separate bowl, mix together flour, baking powder and salt. Add flour mixture to butter mixture, blending well. Stir in extracts. Drop dough by teaspoonfuls onto greased baking sheets. Bake at 375 degrees for 10 minutes, or until just lightly golden. Cool on wire racks; frost with Citrus Icing.

Citrus Icing:
1/4 c. butter, softened
2 c. powdered sugar
3 T. orange or lemon juice
1 T. orange or lemon zest

Blend butter and powdered sugar. Add juice and zest; mix well.

Tiffany Leiter, Midland, MI

Speedy Peanut Butter Cookies

That's correct...there's no flour in these cookies!

Makes one dozen

1 c. sugar
1 c. creamy peanut butter
1 egg, beaten

Blend ingredients together; set aside for 5 minutes. Scoop dough with a small ice cream scoop; place 2 inches apart on ungreased baking sheets. Make a crisscross pattern on top of each cookie using the tines of a fork; bake at 350 degrees for 10 to 12 minutes. Cool on baking sheets for 5 minutes; remove to wire rack to finish cooling.

Speedy Peanut Butter Cookies

Kim Robertson, South Hill, VA

Oatmeal-Raisin Spice Cookies

This cookie can easily be made into a gift mix. Just layer the first four ingredients in a wide-mouth, one-quart canning jar, packing down tightly in between each layer. Sift the next five ingredients and layer over oats. Attach a gift card with this recipe and baking directions.

Makes about 3 dozen

3/4 c. brown sugar, packed
1/2 c. sugar
3/4 c. raisins
2 c. quick-cooking oats, uncooked
1 c. all-purpose flour
1 t. cinnamon
1/4 t. nutmeg
1 t. baking powder
1/2 t. salt
3/4 c. butter, softened
1 egg, beaten
1 t. vanilla extract

Combine dry ingredients in a large mixing bowl. Add butter, egg and vanilla, mixing well. Drop by tablespoonfuls on greased baking sheets. Bake at 350 degrees for 15 minutes, or until edges are golden brown. Cool on wire racks.

Sharon Demers, Dolores, CO

Coconut-Lime Macaroons

These little nuggets of coconut goodness just can't be beat! Our entire family loves them!

Makes 3 dozen

3 egg whites, beaten
3 c. sweetened flaked coconut
1/4 c. sugar
4 T. all-purpose flour
1/4 c. lime juice
1 to 2 T. lime zest
1/4 t. vanilla extract

In a large bowl, combine all ingredients; mix thoroughly. Drop by teaspoonfuls 1/2 inch apart on lightly greased baking sheets. Bake at 350 degrees for 12 to 15 minutes, until edges are lightly golden.

COOKIE KNOW-HOW
Shredded coconut comes sweetened or unsweetened and can be very coarse or finely shredded. Choose the type that fits what your family likes best. Any kind will work and make a delicious cookie.

Coconut-Lime Macaroons

Dorothy Ames, Lerna, IL

Nellie's Persimmon Cookies

A ripe persimmon should be soft to the touch and yield between 1/2 to 3/4 cup of pulp.

Makes 6 dozen

1 persimmon
1 c. butter, softened
1 c. brown sugar, packed
1 c. sugar
2 eggs, beaten
2-1/2 c. all-purpose flour
1/2 t. baking soda
1 c. chopped pecans

Rinse persimmon under cold water; pat dry. Using a small sharp knife, make an X-shaped cut in the pointed end. Pull back sections of peel from cut end; discard seeds, peel and stem end. Process pulp in food processor or blender until smooth. Reserve 1/2 cup persimmon pulp purée; save any remaining pulp purée for another use. Beat butter and sugars in a large bowl with an electric mixer at medium speed until light and fluffy. Beat in eggs and persimmon pulp. Combine flour and baking soda in a separate bowl, stirring to mix. Gradually add flour mixture to butter mixture, beating until blended. Fold in pecans; cover and chill one hour. Drop by teaspoonfuls onto ungreased baking sheets. Press each cookie with a fork dipped in warm water. Bake at 350 degrees for 10 minutes, or until golden. Remove to wire racks to cool. Store in an airtight container.

Brita Greenough, Ankeny, IA

Breakfast Cookies

These cookies are full of goodness and start your day off right.

Makes 4 dozen

2 c. butter, softened
2-1/2 c. brown sugar, packed
1 t. vanilla extract
4 eggs
4-1/4 c. all-purpose flour
1 t. baking powder
2 t. baking soda
1 t. salt
1-1/4 c. old-fashioned oats, uncooked
1/2 c. dried cranberries
1/4 c. slivered almonds
1/2 c. raisin & bran cereal
2 T. orange juice
10-oz. pkg. dark chocolate chips

In a large mixing bowl, beat butter, brown sugar and vanilla extract until creamy. Add eggs, one at a time, beating well after each addition. In a small bowl, combine flour, baking powder, baking soda, salt and oats. Add to butter mixture and beat in gradually. Stir in cranberries, nuts, cereal, orange juice and chips. Drop onto ungreased baking sheets by rounded tablespoonfuls. Bake at 375 degrees for 9 to 11 minutes or until golden. Cool on baking sheets for 2 minutes; remove to wire racks to cool completely.

Breakfast Cookies

Casey Tabolt, Pulaski, NY

Madelene's Buttermilk-Molasses Cookies

My grandmother would make these cookies and then give us a call. We always went right over so we could eat them warm out of the oven!

Makes 2 to 3 dozen

1 c. shortening
1-1/2 c. sugar, divided
1 c. light molasses
1 c. buttermilk
1 t. vanilla extract
5 c. all-purpose flour
4 t. baking soda
1/2 t. salt
1/2 t. ground ginger
1/2 t. cinnamon
Optional: 1 c. raisins

In a bowl, beat shortening, one cup sugar, molasses, buttermilk and vanilla. In another bowl, combine flour, baking soda, salt and spices. Stir flour mixture into shortening mixture; mix in raisins, if desired. Drop dough by rounded teaspoonfuls onto greased baking sheets, 2 inches apart. Sprinkle with remaining sugar to cover. Bake at 350 degrees for 12 to 15 minutes. Cool on wire racks.

Penny Sherman, Ava, MO

Orange Cranberry Cookies

These cookies are perfect for those busy days when you have to rush out the door, but need a little snack to keep you going.

Makes 1-1/2 dozen

1/2 c. butter, softened
1/2 c. sugar
1 egg, beaten
2 T. frozen orange juice concentrate, thawed
1 T. orange zest
1-1/4 c. all-purpose flour
1 t. baking powder
1/2 c. corn flake cereal
1/2 c. dried cranberries

Blend together butter and sugar in a bowl until light and fluffy. Beat in egg, orange juice and zest; set aside. Combine flour and baking powder in a small bowl; stir into butter mixture until blended. Stir in cereal and cranberries. Drop by tablespoonfuls, 2 inches apart, on an ungreased baking sheet. Bake at 350 degrees for 10 to 12 minutes, until golden around edges. Cool on a wire rack.

Orange Cranberry Cookies

Karen Adams, Cincinnati, OH

Granny's Chocolate Fudge Cookies

The sweetened condensed milk in these cookies makes them extra sweet and chewy!

Makes 5 to 6 dozen

14-oz. can sweetened condensed
    milk
12-oz. pkg. semi-sweet chocolate
    chips
1/4 c. butter
1 c. all-purpose flour
1 c. chopped nuts
1 t. vanilla extract

Place condensed milk, chocolate chips and butter in a microwave-safe bowl. Microwave, uncovered, on high, stirring every 30 seconds, until melted. Add flour, nuts and vanilla. Drop by teaspoonfuls onto greased baking sheets. Bake at 350 degrees for 7 minutes. Cool on wire racks.

Debbie Blundi, Kunkletown, PA

"Free" Coconut Cookies

I call these my "free" cookies because they are sugar-free, fat-free and dairy-free.

Makes 1-1/4 dozen

8 pitted dates
1 very ripe banana, sliced
1-1/2 c. unsweetened flaked coconut
1/8 t. vanilla extract
1/8 t. pumpkin pie spice

Place dates in a small bowl; add enough water to cover. Let stand for 2 to 4 hours; drain. Place dates, banana, coconut, vanilla and spice in a food processor or blender. Process until smooth and mixture resembles cookie dough. If mixture is too dry, add a drop or 2 of water; if mixture is too sticky, add a little more coconut. Scoop dough by teaspoonfuls onto ungreased baking sheets, one inch apart. Bake at 325 degrees for 10 to 15 minutes, until tips of coconut start to brown on the bottom; cookies will not brown on top. Let cookies stand on baking sheet until cool; remove to a plate. Leave uncovered for the first day, so cookies don't get too moist.

"Free" Coconut Cookies

Dottie McCraw, Oklahoma City, OK

White Chocolate Macaroons

Ready-made cookie dough makes these super simple.

Makes 2 dozen cookies

18-oz. tube refrigerated white chocolate chunk cookie dough, at room temperature
2-1/4 c. sweetened flaked coconut
2 t. vanilla extract
1/2 t. coconut extract

Combine all ingredients; mix well. Drop by rounded teaspoonfuls onto ungreased baking sheets; bake at 350 degrees for 10 to 12 minutes. Cool on baking sheets for 2 minutes; remove to wire rack to cool completely.

Lucille Mitten, Goldfield, IA

Healthy Morning Cookies

The spices in these oatmeal cookies makes them extra good! They are hearty and not too sweet, so they make a great breakfast cookie. Cutting them into half-circles makes them seem like a tasty hand-pie... perfect to grab and go!

Makes about 2 dozen cookie halves

1 t. baking soda
2 T. hot water
1 c. butter
1 c. sugar
2 eggs, beaten
2 c. all-purpose flour
1 t. baking powder
1/2 t. salt
1 t. cinnamon
1/2 t. ground cloves
1/4 t. nutmeg
1 t. orange zest
2-1/2 c. old-fashioned oats, uncooked
1/2 c. chopped walnuts
1/2 c. chopped pecans
1/2 c. sweetened, dried cranberries
1/4 c. dried apricots, chopped
1/4 c. candied orange peel, chopped

Dissolve baking soda in hot water; set aside. In a large bowl, blend butter and sugar. Add eggs and baking soda mixture; stir well. Add flour, baking powder, salt, spices and orange zest; mix well. Stir in remaining ingredients. Drop by tablespoons onto parchment-lined baking sheets. Bake at 350 degrees for about 20 minutes. Cool for 5 minutes; cut each cookie in half if desired. Cool on a wire rack.

Healthy Morning Cookies

Penny Sherman, Cumming, GA

Grab & Go Breakfast Cookies

These cookies are perfect for those busy mornings when you have to rush out the door.

Makes 1-1/2 dozen

1/2 c. butter, softened
1/2 c. sugar
1 egg, beaten
2 T. frozen orange juice concentrate, thawed
1 T. orange zest
1-1/4 c. all-purpose flour
1 t. baking powder
1/2 c. wheat & barley cereal

Blend together butter and sugar in a bowl until light and fluffy. Beat in egg, orange juice and zest; set aside. Combine flour and baking powder in a small bowl; stir into butter mixture until blended. Stir in cereal. Drop by tablespoonfuls, 2 inches apart, on an ungreased baking sheet. Bake at 350 degrees for 10 to 12 minutes, until golden around edges. Cool on a wire rack.

Diana Carlile, Chatham, IL

Oatmeal-Carrot Cookies

These chewy cookies are my family's favorites!

Makes 3 dozen

3/4 c. butter, softened
3/4 c. brown sugar, packed
1/2 c. sugar
1-3/4 c. all-purpose flour, divided
1 egg, beaten
1 t. baking powder
1/4 t. baking soda
1/2 t. cinnamon
1 t. vanilla extract
2 c. quick-cooking oats, uncooked
1 c. carrots, peeled and shredded
Optional: 1/2 c. raisins

Beat butter until soft. Add sugars and 1/2 cup flour; mix well. Add remaining ingredients except oats, carrots and raisins. Beat well. Add remaining flour; mix well. Stir in oats, carrots and raisins, if using. Drop by rounded teaspoonfuls onto ungreased baking sheets. Bake at 375 degrees for 10 minutes.

Oatmeal-Carrot Cookies

Carol Field Dahlstrom, Ankeny, IA

Carol's Famous Chocolate Chip Cookies

I can't make these fast enough for all the grandchildren...and for my husband and I too!

Makes 4 dozen cookies

2 c. butter
1-1/2 c. brown sugar, packed
1-1/2 c. sugar
1 t. salt
1 t. vanilla
4 eggs
4-1/2 c. flour
2 t. baking soda
1 c. old-fashioned oats, uncooked
1 T. water
2 10-oz. pkg. dark chocolate chips
Optional: 3/4 c. chopped nuts

In a large bowl, beat butter and sugars until creamy. Add salt and vanilla. Add eggs, one at a time, beating well after each addition. In a small bowl, mix flour, baking soda and oats. Beat in flour mixture gradually. Stir in chocolate chips and nuts if using. Drop onto parchment paper-lined baking sheets by rounded tablespoonfuls. Bake at 375 degrees for about 10 minutes or until golden brown. Cool on baking sheets for 2 minutes; remove to wire racks to cool completely.

Brenda Melancon, Gonzales, LA

Lemon-Macadamia Cookies

My daughter loves macadamia nuts, and I love lemon, so I created these scrumptious cookies.

Makes 4 dozen

3/4 c. butter, softened
1 c. sugar
1 c. brown sugar, packed
2 eggs
3.4-oz. pkg. instant lemon pudding mix
2-1/4 c. all-purpose flour
1 t. baking soda
1/4 t. salt
2 t. lemon zest
1 t. lemon extract
1 c. macadamia nuts, coarsely chopped
1/2 c. toffee baking bits

In a large bowl, combine butter and sugars. Beat with an electric mixer on medium speed until light and fluffy. Add eggs, one at a time, beating well after each addition; set aside. Combine dry pudding mix, flour, baking soda, salt and zest in a separate bowl. Slowly add pudding mixture to butter mixture. Add extract; beat until combined. Stir in nuts and toffee bits. Drop dough by rounded tablespoonfuls onto ungreased baking sheets, 2 inches apart. Bake at 350 degrees for 10 to 12 minutes, until lightly golden around edges. Cool cookies on baking sheets for 2 minutes. Remove to wire racks to cool completely. Store in an airtight container.

Lemon-Macadamia Cookies

Michelle Sheridan, Upper Arlington, OH

Chocolate Chip Tea Cookies

These little cookies look so pretty yet are easy to make. You can make them bigger if you like, but the size of these makes them more like a tea cookie.

Makes about 4 dozen

1 c. butter, softened
1/2 c. powdered sugar
1 t. vanilla extract
2 c. all-purpose flour
1-1/2 c. mini semi-sweet chocolate
   chips, divided

With an electric mixer on high speed, beat butter and powdered sugar until fluffy. Add vanilla; mix well. Gradually beat in flour; use a spoon to stir in one cup chocolate chips. Drop by teaspoonfuls 2 inches apart on ungreased baking sheets. Bake at 350 degrees for 10 to 12 minutes. Remove to wire rack to cool. Place remaining chocolate chips in a small plastic zipping bag. Seal bag; microwave on high until melted, about 30 seconds. Snip off a small corner of bag; drizzle chocolate over cooled cookies. Chill for 5 minutes, or until chocolate is set.

Kathy Grashoff, Fort Wayne, IN

Espresso Bean Cookies

You can find chocolate-covered coffee beans in various package sizes at most coffee shops. One 6-ounce package equals about one cup.

Makes 4 dozen

1 c. butter, softened
3/4 c. brown sugar, packed
1/4 c. sugar
2 eggs
1 t. vanilla extract
2-1/4 c. all-purpose flour
1 t. baking soda
1 t. salt
1/2 t. cinnamon
1 c. chopped almonds, toasted
1 c. chocolate-covered coffee beans
4 1.4-oz. toffee candy bars, chopped

Beat butter with an electric mixer at medium speed until creamy. Gradually add sugars, beating well after each addition. Add eggs, one at a time, beating until blended after each addition; add vanilla, and beat until blended. Combine flour, baking soda, salt and cinnamon in a separate bowl. Gradually add flour mixture to butter mixture, beating well. Stir in almonds, coffee beans and chopped candy bars. Cover and chill dough until firm. Drop by teaspoonfuls onto ungreased baking sheets. Bake at 350 degrees for 10 to 11 minutes, until golden. Cool on pans one minute; remove to wire racks to cool completely. Store in an airtight container.

Espresso Bean Cookies

Charlene Sidwell, Altamont, IL

Frosted Cherry Drops

These have always been a favorite of our family. They're perfect for a colorful plate of cookies, either for home or as a gift.

Makes 2-1/2 to 3 dozen

18-1/2-oz. pkg. white cake mix
1/2 c. sour cream
1 egg, beaten
1/4 t. almond extract
3 T. maraschino cherry juice
1/2 c. maraschino cherries, finely
    chopped
Garnish: maraschino cherries,
    quartered

In a bowl, combine dry cake mix, sour cream, egg, extract and cherry juice; beat well. Fold in chopped cherries. Drop by teaspoonfuls onto ungreased baking sheets, 2 inches apart. Bake at 350 degrees for 8 to 12 minutes, until edges are lightly golden. Cool for one minute on baking sheets; remove to wire racks to cool completely. Frost with Cherry Frosting; top with quartered cherries.

Cherry Frosting:
2-1/2 c. powdered sugar
1/4 c. butter, softened
1 T. maraschino cherry juice
2 to 3 T. milk

Combine all ingredients in a bowl; stir until smooth.

Trudy Cox, Plano, TX

The Best Oatmeal Cookies

The name of this recipe says it all! This is a recipe I received from a friend back in 1989.

Makes 4 dozen

1 c. golden raisins
3 eggs, beaten
1 t. vanilla extract
1 c. butter, softened
1 c. brown sugar, packed
1 c. sugar
2-1/2 c. all-purpose flour
1 t. salt
2 t. baking soda
1 T. cinnamon
2 c. quick-cooking oats, uncooked
1 c. chopped pecans

In a small bowl, combine raisins, eggs and vanilla. Cover with plastic wrap and let stand one hour. In a large bowl, combine butter and sugars. In a separate bowl, whisk together flour, salt, baking soda and cinnamon. Add flour mixture to butter mixture; mix until well blended. Stir in raisin mixture, oats and pecans. Dough will be stiff. Drop by rounded teaspoonfuls onto ungreased baking sheets. Bake at 350 degrees for 10 to 12 minutes.

The Best Oatmeal Cookies

Emily's Gingerbread Cookies, p. 164

CHAPTER SIX

Cut-Out
Cookies

Easiest-Ever Sugar Cookies, p. 170

Good Neighbor Sugar Cookies, p. 156

Diana Hamilton, Beaverton, OR

Good Neighbor Sugar Cookies

These are the best sugar cookies ever! You can make them for any holiday or just for a special treat.

Makes about 3 dozen

3 c. all-purpose flour
1 t. cream of tartar
1 t. baking soda
1 t. salt
3/4 c. butter
2 eggs, beaten
1 c. sugar
1 t. vanilla extract

Mix together flour, cream of tartar, baking soda and salt in a bowl. In a separate bowl, whisk together remaining ingredients with a fork. Stir butter mixture into flour mixture. Wrap dough in plastic wrap; refrigerate for 30 minutes. On a floured surface, roll out dough 1/8-inch thick; cut out with cookie cutters. Arrange on lightly greased baking sheets. Bake at 375 degrees for 5 to 6 minutes, until lightly golden. Cool. Frost using one tablespoon of frosting per cookie. Decorate as desired.

Powdered Sugar Frosting:
3 c. powdered sugar
2 T. butter, melted
3 T. milk

Mix all ingredients together until smooth.

COOKIE KNOW-HOW
When using cookie cutters, always dip the cutter in flour or powdered sugar before cutting. It will make them cut cleaner without sticking.

Good Neighbor Sugar Cookies

Sue Ellen Morrison, Blue Springs, MO

Spirited Raisin Cookies

These cookies smell wonderful while baking...the taste is out of this world! My mother kept these on hand as an after-school treat.

Makes about one dozen

1/2 c. water
3 T. rum extract
1 c. raisins
1 c. butter, softened
1/2 c. powdered sugar
2 c. all-purpose flour
1/4 t. baking powder
1/4 t. salt

In a small saucepan over low heat, combine water, extract and raisins. Bring to a boil; remove from heat. Cover and let stand 30 minutes; drain. In a large bowl, blend butter and powdered sugar; set aside. In a separate bowl, mix flour, baking powder and salt; gradually stir into butter mixture. Fold in raisins. Roll out dough on a floured surface to 1/2-inch thick. Cut with cookie cutters, as desired. Place cookies on ungreased baking sheets. Bake at 375 degrees for 20 minutes. Cool on a wire rack.

Jennie Gist, Gooseberry Patch

Gingerbread Cookies

The spicy aroma of these cookies baking will get you in the Christmas spirit! And you'll love decorating with Royal Icing...it sets up "hard" so the cookies can be handled.

Makes 2 dozen

1/2 c. butter, softened
1/2 c. brown sugar, packed
1/2 c. molasses
1 egg, beaten
3 c. all-purpose flour
1-1/2 t. cinnamon
1 t. ground ginger
1/4 t. baking powder
1/4 t. baking soda
1/2 t. salt
Royal Icing (see page 94)

Combine butter and brown sugar in a large bowl. Beat with an electric mixer on medium speed until fluffy. Beat in molasses and egg; set aside. In a separate bowl, combine remaining ingredients except Royal icing; mix well. Stir flour mixture into butter mixture. Wrap dough in plastic wrap; chill for one hour. Roll out on a lightly floured surface to 1/8-inch thickness. Cut out dough with cookie cutters as desired; place on ungreased baking sheets. Bake at 350 degrees for 10 to 12 minutes, until lightly golden. Transfer cookies to a wire rack to cool. Decorate with Royal Icing.

Gingerbread Cookies

Judee DeVine, Venetia, PA

Dipped Gingerbread Stars

Spicy and sweet with a jacket of chocolate...they're irresistible!

Makes about 5 dozen

1 c. shortening
1 c. brown sugar, packed
3/4 c. molasses
3/4 c. buttermilk
2 eggs, beaten
4-1/2 c. all-purpose flour
1 T. ground ginger
2 t. baking soda
1 t. salt
Garnish: white and/or semi-sweet
    chocolate chips, melted

In a large bowl, blend shortening and brown sugar. Add molasses, buttermilk and eggs; stir well and set aside. In a separate bowl, mix flour, ginger, baking soda and salt. Blend flour mixture into shortening mixture. Mix well; cover and refrigerate overnight. Roll out dough 1/4-inch thick on a lightly floured surface; cut out with a star cookie cutter. Arrange on ungreased baking sheets. Bake at 400 degrees for 10 to 12 minutes. Let cool completely; dip half of each cookie into melted chocolate. Place cookies on wax paper to set.

Meri Hebert, Cheboygan, MI

Buttermilk Sugar Cookies

I make these for every holiday... they're the softest cookies ever, and everyone always wants the recipe!

Makes about 6 dozen

2 c. shortening
2 c. sugar
4 eggs, beaten
1 T. vanilla extract
2 c. buttermilk
6 c. all-purpose flour
1 T. plus 1 t. baking powder
2 t. baking soda
1/2 t. salt
16-oz. container favorite frosting
Optional: candy sprinkles

In a large bowl, blend together shortening, sugar, eggs and vanilla. Add buttermilk and mix well. In a separate bowl, combine flour, baking powder, baking soda and salt; stir into shortening mixture. Add more flour if needed to make a firm dough. Cover and chill for 2 to 3 hours or overnight. On a floured surface, roll out dough 1/4-inch thick. Cut with cookie cutters; place on greased baking sheets. Bake at 350 degrees for 7 to 8 minutes. Cool on wire racks. Frost and decorate as desired.

Buttermilk Sugar Cookies

Henry Burnley, Ankeny, IA

Best Sugar Cookies

I love these cookies and I make them with my Grandma. So much fun!

Makes about 3 dozen

1 c. butter, softened
2 c. sugar
3 eggs, beaten
1 t. almond extract
5-1/2 c. all-purpose flour
1 t. baking soda
1/2 t. salt
1/3 c. milk

Blend butter and sugar together; stir in eggs and almond extract. Beat well. In a small bowl, mix flour, soda and salt. Mix in alternately with milk. Mix until well blended. Shape dough into a ball; cover and chill for 4 hours to overnight. Roll out dough 1/4-inch thick on a lightly floured surface; cut with cookie cutters as desired. Arrange cookies on lightly greased baking sheets. Bake at 350 degrees for 8 to 10 minutes, until golden. Cool completely; frost with Powdered Sugar Frosting (see at right). Decorate as desired.

Tina Knotts, Cable, OH

Quick Sugar Cookies

Everyone needs a dependable sugar cookie recipe...this is mine. I roll them out and cut them in squares when I am in a hurry. Then I just drizzle frosting over them all. So easy!

Makes 4 dozen

2 c. butter, softened
1-1/3 c. brown sugar, packed
2 eggs, beaten
2 t. vanilla extract
5 c. all-purpose flour

In a large bowl, blend butter and sugar together; stir in eggs and vanilla. Add flour; mix until well blended. Shape dough into a ball; chill in freezer for 10 minutes. Roll out dough 1/4-inch thick on a lightly floured surface. Transfer to parchment paper-lined baking sheet and cut into squares. Or, roll out and cut out with cookie cutters as desired. Bake at 350 degrees for 8 to 10 minutes, until golden. Cool on wire racks. Frost cookies when cool by drizzling or spreading with Powdered Sugar Frosting.

Powdered Sugar Frosting:
4-1/2 c. powdered sugar
6 T. butter, melted
6 T. milk
2 T. vanilla extract
1 T. lemon juice

Combine all ingredients in a medium bowl. Beat with an electric mixer on low speed until smooth.

Quick Sugar Cookies

Sonna Johnson, Goldfield, IA

Emily's Gingerbread Cookies

There are so many great gingerbread cookie recipes. This is our favorite. Because we live on a farm, I love to make these in animal shapes. The kids love them! The cookie dough rolls out so well that you can use cookie cutters that have thinner spaces. With some cookie recipes, this does not work well.

Makes about 3 dozen

1/3 c. brown sugar, packed
1/3 c. shortening
2/3 c. molasses
1 egg, beaten
3 c. all-purpose flour
1 T. baking powder
1-1/2 t. ground ginger
1/2 t. salt

Blend together brown sugar and shortening until light and fluffy. Beat in molasses. Add egg, beating well. In a separate bowl, sift together flour, baking powder, ginger and salt. Add flour mixture to sugar mixture; mix well. Cover and refrigerate for 2 hours. Divide dough into fourths. On a floured surface, roll out to 1/4-inch thickness. Cut with cookie cutters. Place on greased baking sheets. Bake at 350 degrees for 5 to 7 minutes, until dark golden. Cool slightly on pans before removing to wire racks to cool completely. Decorate with Frosting as desired.

Frosting:

2-1/2 c. powdered sugar
3 T. butter, melted
3 T. milk
1 T. vanilla extract
1 t. lemon juice

Combine all ingredients in a medium bowl. Beat with an electric mixer on low speed until smooth.

Emily's Gingerbread Cookies

Amy Butcher, Columbus, GA

Butterscotch Gingerbread Cookies

The pudding in these cookies is always a surprise when you see it in the ingredients list. But it surely makes the cookies soft and yummy!

Makes about one dozen

1/2 c. butter, softened
1/2 c. brown sugar, packed
3.5-oz. pkg. cook & serve
    butterscotch pudding mix
1 egg, beaten
1-1/2 c. all-purpose flour
1-1/2 t. ground ginger
1 t. cinnamon
1/2 t. baking soda

Beat butter, brown sugar and pudding mix in a large bowl with an electric mixer at medium speed until light and fluffy; add egg and beat well. Combine flour, ginger, cinnamon and baking soda in a separate bowl, stirring to mix. Gradually stir flour mixture into butter mixture, mixing until blended. Chill 30 minutes. Roll dough in batches to 1/4-inch thickness on a floured surface; cut with cookie cutters as desired. Place on a greased baking sheet and bake at 350 degrees for 8 to 10 minutes, until golden. Remove to a wire rack to cool completely. Store in an airtight container.

Lillian Dahlstrom, Ames, IA

Swig Cookies

This makes a quick small-batch of yummy cookies. Roll them thick and cut them out. Or sometimes, when I am in a hurry, I drop them instead.

Makes 2 dozen

2 c. all-purpose flour
1/2 t. cream of tartar
3/4 t. baking soda
1/2 t. salt
1/2 c. butter, softened
1 eggs, beaten
3/4 c. sugar
1 t. almond extract
Garnish: candy sprinkles

Mix together flour, cream of tartar, baking soda and salt in a bowl. In a separate bowl, whisk together remaining ingredients with a fork. Stir butter mixture into flour mixture. Wrap dough in plastic wrap; refrigerate for 30 minutes. On a floured surface, roll out dough 1/4-inch thick; cut out with cookie cutters. Arrange on lightly greased baking sheets. Bake at 375 degrees for 5 to 6 minutes, until lightly golden. Cool. Frost using one tablespoon of frosting per cookie. Decorate as desired.

Simple Powdered Sugar Frosting:
2 c. powdered sugar
1 T. butter, melted
2 T. whole milk

Mix all ingredients together until smooth.

Swig Cookies

Diane Axtell, Marble Falls, TX

Homemade Graham Crackers

These cookie-like crackers are a treat!

Makes 4 dozen

1/2 c. butter, softened
3/4 c. brown sugar, packed
1 t. vanilla extract
2 c. whole-wheat flour
1 c. all-purpose flour
1 t. baking powder
1/2 t. baking soda
1/8 t. salt
3/4 c. milk
cinnamon to taste

Beat butter and brown sugar in a large bowl with an electric mixer at medium speed until fluffy; add vanilla and beat until blended. Combine flours, baking powder, baking soda and salt in a separate bowl, stirring to mix. Gradually add flour mixture to butter mixture alternately with milk, beginning and ending with flour mixture, beating after each addition. Cover dough and chill one hour, or until firm.

Roll dough to 1/8-inch thickness on a lightly floured surface; cut into 2-inch rectangles and sprinkle with cinnamon. Place crackers 1/2 inch apart on greased baking sheets. Bake at 350 degrees for 10 to 12 minutes, until edges are golden. Remove to wire racks to cool. Store in an airtight container. Makes 4 dozen.

Lynda Robson, Boston, MA

Gingerbread Babies

Tuck them into a little box and leave them on someone's doorstep...surely you know someone who will give them a good home any time of year!

Makes about 12 dozen

3/4 c. butter, softened
3/4 c. brown sugar, packed
1 egg, beaten
1/2 c. dark molasses
2-2/3 c. all-purpose flour
2 t. ground ginger
1/2 t ground allspice
1/2 t. nutmeg
1/2 t. cinnamon
1/4 t. salt

In a large bowl, blend together butter and brown sugar until fluffy. Add egg and molasses. In a separate bowl, combine remaining ingredients; gradually stir into butter mixture. Turn dough out onto a well-floured surface; roll out to 1/8-inch thickness. Cut dough with a 2-inch gingerbread boy cookie cutter. Place on greased baking sheets. Bake at 350 degrees for 9 to 10 minutes, until firm.

Gingerbread Babies

Barbara Schmeckpeper, Minooka, IL

Raisin-Filled Cookies

My grandmother did so many special things. She always served hot chocolate to us children along with these delicious cookies. What fond memories!

Makes 1-1/2 to 2 dozen

1 c. shortening
1 c. sugar
1 c. brown sugar, packed
3 eggs, beaten
1 t. vanilla extract
4 c. all-purpose flour
1 t. baking soda
1/2 t. salt

In a large bowl, mix together all ingredients until well combined. Roll out dough on a lightly floured surface, 1/4-inch thick. Cut with a 2-inch round cookie cutter. Spread Raisin Filling onto half the cookies; top with remaining cookies. Press edges with a fork dipped in flour to seal. Place on greased baking sheets. Bake at 350 degrees for 9 to 10 minutes. Cool on wire racks.

Raisin Filling:
1-1/2 c. raisins, finely chopped
1/2 c. water
1 T. sugar
1 T. all-purpose flour

Mix together all ingredients in a saucepan over medium heat. Bring to a boil, stirring often. Remove from heat; cool slightly.

Virginia Watson, Scranton, PA

Easiest-Ever Sugar Cookies

So easy to mix up, even the kids can help...and of course, they will want to!

Makes 2 to 3 dozen

3.4-oz. pkg. instant vanilla pudding
    mix
1/2 c. sugar
1/2 c. butter, softened
1 egg, beaten
1-1/2 c. all-purpose flour
1 t. baking powder
Optional: sanding sugar, candy
    sprinkles

Blend together dry pudding mix, sugar and butter; stir in egg and set aside. In a separate bowl, combine flour and baking powder; blend thoroughly into pudding mixture. Cover and chill until firm. Roll out dough 1/8-inch to 1/4-inch thick on a lightly floured surface; cut with desired cookie cutters. Place on lightly greased baking sheets. Bake at 350 degrees for 8 to 9 minutes. When cool, frost and decorate as desired.

Easiest-Ever Sugar Cookies

Peanut Butter-Oat Bars, p.208

CHAPTER SEVEN

Beautiful Bar Cookies

Apple Brownies, p. 198

Double-Berry Nut Bars, p. 204

Kelly Wood, Salem, OH

Grandma Gray's Spice-Nut Bars

This recipe belonged to my great-grandmother on my mother's side. Mother made these cookie bars every Christmas...we always gobbled them up immediately.

Makes 2 dozen

1-1/2 c. all-purpose flour
1/2 t. baking powder
1/2 t. baking soda
1/2 t. salt
1/2 t. cinnamon
1/4 t. nutmeg
1/8 t. ground cloves
1/4 c. butter, softened
1 c. brown sugar, packed
1 egg, beaten
1/2 c. plus 1 T. hot coffee, divided
1/2 c. raisins
1/2 c. chopped walnuts
1/2 c. powdered sugar

Combine flour, baking powder, baking soda, salt, cinnamon, nutmeg and cloves in a large bowl; mix. Beat butter, brown sugar and egg in a separate large bowl with an electric mixer at medium speed until blended. Add 1/2 cup coffee and beat well; stir in raisins and walnuts. Gradually add flour mixture to butter mixture. Pour mixture into a greased 13"x9" baking pan. Bake at 350 degrees for 20 to 25 minutes, until golden. Combine powdered sugar and remaining coffee in a small bowl; stir well. Immediately spread glaze over warm bars. Cool in pan on a wire rack and cut into bars.

Janet Seabern, Winona, MN

Snowy Glazed Apple Squares

My mother used to make this dessert when I was a young girl. It is our family favorite!

Makes 2 dozen

2-1/2 c. all-purpose flour
1/2 t. salt
1 c. shortening
2 eggs, separated
1/2 to 2/3 c. milk
1-1/2 c. corn flake cereal, crushed
8 baking apples, peeled, cored
   and sliced
1 c. sugar
1 t. cinnamon
2 T. powdered sugar

In a bowl, mix flour and salt; cut in shortening. Beat egg yolks in a measuring cup; add enough milk to measure 2/3 cup. Add to flour mixture and mix lightly. Divide dough into 2 parts, one slightly larger than the other. Roll out larger portion into a 15-inch by 10-inch rectangle. Place on a lightly greased 15"x10" jelly-roll pan. Sprinkle evenly with cereal; arrange apple slices over cereal. Mix sugar and cinnamon; sprinkle over apples. Roll out remaining dough and place on top; seal edges and cut slits in top. Beat egg whites until foamy and spread over dough. Bake at 350 degrees for one hour. Cool slightly; sift powdered sugar over top. Cut into squares.

Snowy Glazed Apple Squares

Joan White, Malvern, PA

Staycation Coconut-Lime Bars

A tangy dessert that puts you in the mood for sandy beaches and warm breezes!

Makes 4 dozen

2 c. all-purpose flour
1/4 c. sugar
1/8 t. salt
1/2 c. plus 2-1/2 T. butter
4 eggs, beaten
1 c. chopped almonds
2 c. brown sugar, packed
3 c. sweetened flaked coconut
1-1/2 c. powdered sugar
2 T. lime juice
2 t. lime zest

Combine flour, sugar and salt in a bowl. Cut in butter until mixture resembles coarse meal. Press into an ungreased 15"x10" jelly-roll pan. Bake at 350 degrees for 15 minutes, or until golden. Meanwhile, mix eggs, almonds, brown sugar and coconut until well blended; spread over crust. Bake an additional 30 minutes, or until set. Remove pan to a wire rack; loosen the edges with a metal spatula. Use a fork to combine powdered sugar, lime juice and zest. Working quickly, spread powdered sugar mixture over top while still warm. Let cool; cut into bars.

Wendy Ball, Battle Creek, MI

Peach Mango Melba Shortbread Bars

I made a pan of these bars for a day of scrapbooking at a friend's church... they were a big hit! If you can't find peach mango preserves, plain peach preserves can be substituted.

Makes 2 to 3 dozen

2 c. all-purpose flour
1/2 c. sugar
1/4 t. salt
1 c. cold butter, cubed
1 c. peach mango preserves, large chunks cut up
1/2 c. red raspberry jam
1/2 c. slivered almonds, lightly toasted
3/4 c. powdered sugar
1 t. vanilla extract
1 to 2 T. whipping cream or milk

Lightly spray a 9"x9" baking pan with non-stick vegetable spray; set aside. Combine flour, sugar and salt in a bowl. Cut in butter with a pastry blender until crumbly. Reserve one cup of flour mixture; press remaining flour mixture into pan. Bake at 350 degrees for about 20 minutes, until golden. Remove from oven. Spread preserves over warm crust. Spread jam over the preserves. Sprinkle reserved flour mixture over jam layer. Sprinkle with almonds. Return to oven for about 30 minutes, until golden and preserves are slightly bubbly. Set pan on a wire rack to cool. In a separate bowl, combine powdered sugar, vanilla and milk. Whisk until blended to a glaze consistency; drizzle over bars. Cool completely; cut into bars.

Peach Mango Melba Shortbread Bars

Brenda Smith, Delaware, OH

Choco-Berry Goodie Bars

It's so easy to change these yummy Choco-Berry Goodie Bars to suit your family's taste...try using chopped walnuts or pecans instead of almonds and chopped, dried apricots. Or add dark, regular-size chocolate chips instead of mini chocolate chips for a more chocolatey flavor.

Makes 2 dozen

3 c. quick-cooking oats, uncooked
14-oz. can sweetened condensed
    milk
1 c. sweetened flaked coconut
1 c. sliced almonds
1 c. mini semi-sweet chocolate chips
1/2 c. sweetened dried cranberries
2 T. butter, melted

Combine all ingredients in a large bowl; use your hands to mix well. Press into a greased 13"x9" baking pan. Bake at 350 degrees for 20 to 25 minutes, until edges are golden. Cool 5 minutes; slice into squares and cool completely. Store in an airtight container.

Lisa Thomsen, Rapid City, SD

Gail's Pumpkin Bars

These moist, full-of-flavor pumpkin bars are wonderful in the fall but are appreciated any time of year!

Makes 3 dozen

4 eggs, beaten
3/4 c. oil
1-1/2 c. sugar
15-oz. can pumpkin
2 c. all-purpose flour
2 t. baking powder
1 t. baking soda
1/2 t. salt
2 t. cinnamon
1/2 t. ground ginger
1/2 t. nutmeg
1/2 t. ground cloves

Mix together eggs, oil, sugar and pumpkin in a large bowl. Add remaining ingredients and mix well; pour into a greased and floured 18"x 12" jelly-roll pan. Bake at 350 degrees for 30 to 40 minutes, until a toothpick comes out clean. Let cool; frost with Cream Cheese Frosting and cut into bars.

Cream Cheese Frosting:
3 T. cream cheese, softened
1 T. butter, softened
2 T. milk
1 t. vanilla extract
2 c. powdered sugar

Beat together cream cheese, butter, milk and vanilla; gradually stir in powdered sugar and mix until spreading consistency.

Gail's Pumpkin Bars

Barbara Wise, Jamestown, OH

Applesauce Spice Bars

These are little nuggets of flavor...you will love them!

Makes 2-1/2 to 3 dozen

2/3 c. brown sugar, packed
1 c. all-purpose flour
1 t. baking soda
1/2 t. salt
1 t. pumpkin pie spice
1 c. applesauce
1/4 c. butter, softened
1 egg
Optional: 1 c. raisins

Combine all ingredients and raisins, if desired, in a large bowl; mix thoroughly. Spread batter in a lightly greased 13"x9" baking pan. Bake at 350 degrees for 25 minutes, or until a toothpick inserted in center comes out clean. Cool completely in pan on a wire rack; frost with Browned Butter Frosting. Cut into 3"x 1" bars.

Browned Butter Frosting:
3 T. butter
1-1/2 c. powdered sugar
1 to 1-1/2 T. milk
1 t. vanilla extract

Melt butter in a medium saucepan over medium heat until light brown in color; remove from heat. Blend in remaining ingredients; beat with an electric mixer at medium speed until frosting is smooth and spreading consistency.

Rhonda Reeder, Ellicott City, MD

Gooey Toffee Scotchies

I'm always looking for desserts with toffee in them. These delectable bars are my new favorites!

Makes 2-1/2 dozen

18-1/2 oz. pkg. yellow cake mix
1/2 c. brown sugar, packed
1/2 c. butter, melted and slightly cooled
2 eggs, beaten
1 c. cashews, chopped
8-oz. pkg. toffee baking bits

In a bowl, beat dry cake mix, brown sugar, butter and eggs with an electric mixer on medium speed for one minute. Stir in cashews. Press mixture into the bottom of a greased 15"x10" jelly-roll pan; sprinkle with toffee bits. Bake at 350 degrees for 15 to 20 minutes, until a toothpick inserted in center comes out clean. Cool in pan and cut into bars or triangles. At serving time, drizzle with warm Toffee Sauce.

Toffee Sauce:
3/4 c. plus 1 T. dark brown sugar, packed
2 T. dark corn syrup
6 T. butter
2/3 c. whipping cream

Bring sugar, syrup and butter to a boil in a saucepan over medium heat. Cook for 2 minutes. Carefully stir in cream and simmer for 2 more minutes, or until sauce thickens. Keep warm.

Gooey Toffee Scotchies

Marcy Richardson, Robbinsdale, MN

Salted Nut Squares

These little gems are just like eating a candy bar. They are so easy to make and everyone loves them!

Makes 2 dozen

16-oz. jar dry-roasted peanuts, divided
1/4 c. butter
10-oz. pkg. peanut butter chips
14-oz. can sweetened condensed milk
10-1/2 oz. pkg. marshmallows

Spread half of peanuts in a lightly greased 13"x9" baking pan. Combine butter, peanut butter chips and condensed milk in a saucepan over medium heat; stir until melted and well blended. Stir in marshmallows until melted; spread marshmallow mixture over peanuts. Sprinkle remaining peanuts over top; gently press down into marshmallow mixture. Cool; chill until set, about one hour. Slice into squares.

Jo Ann, Gooseberry Patch

Cranberry Crumb Bars

We can't wait 'til Christmas for these sweet-tart bar cookies...they've become a tradition! But sometimes we make them for other special occasions too. They are good any time of year!

Makes one dozen

1-1/2 c. plus 1/3 c. all-purpose flour, divided
1/3 c. powdered sugar
1 c. chilled butter, divided
8-oz. pkg. cream cheese, softened
14-oz. can sweetened condensed milk
1/4 c. lemon juice
2 T. cornstarch
3 T. brown sugar, packed and divided
16-oz. can whole-berry cranberry sauce
3/4 c. chopped walnuts

Combine 1-1/2 cups flour and powdered sugar; cut in 3/4 cup butter until crumbly. Press mixture into a greased 13"x9" baking pan. Bake at 350 degrees for 15 to 20 minutes; cool. Beat cream cheese, condensed milk and lemon juice; spread over baked crust. Combine cornstarch and one tablespoon brown sugar; stir in cranberry sauce. Spread over cream cheese layer and set aside. Combine remaining brown sugar and flour, butter and nuts; sprinkle over filling. Bake at 325 degrees for 40 to 45 minutes, until golden. Cool in pan on a wire rack; chill for 3 hours before slicing.

Cranberry Crumb Bars

Delinda Blakney, Scottshill, TN

Dorothy's Raisin Bars

This is one of my mom's favorite recipes! Perfect for packing in lunches or taking along on road trips.

Makes 1-1/4 dozen

1 c. raisins
3/4 c. apple juice
2 T. shortening
1 c. all-purpose flour
1/2 t. salt
1/2 t. baking soda
1/2 t. baking powder
1 t. cinnamon
1/4 t. ground cloves
1/8 t. nutmeg
Optional: 1/4 c. chopped nuts

In a small saucepan over low heat, bring raisins, apple juice and shortening to a boil. Remove from heat and cool. Mix remaining ingredients in a bowl; stir in raisin mixture. Pour mixture into a greased 8"x8" baking pan. Bake at 350 degrees for 35 to 40 minutes; remove from oven and cool. Cut into squares; store in an airtight container.

Jay Wilde, West Des Moines, IA

Chewy Gingerbread Bars

These chewy molasses bars are a treat with a cup of hot tea on a wintry evening.

Makes 2 dozen

4-1/2 c. all-purpose flour
2 t. baking soda
3 t. ground ginger
1-1/2 t. cinnamon
1/4 t. salt
1-1/2 c. butter, softened
2 c. sugar
2 eggs, beaten
1/2 c. molasses
1/2 c. coarse sugar

Coat a 15"x10" baking pan with non-stick cooking spray or line with parchment paper. In a medium bowl, stir together flour, baking soda, spices and salt. In a large bowl, beat butter with an electric mixer on low speed for 30 seconds. Gradually add sugar. Beat until combined, scraping bowl as needed. Beat in eggs and molasses. Beat in as much of the flour mixture as you can with the mixer. Stir in any remaining flour mixture. Pat dough into the prepared pan. Sprinkle with coarse sugar. Bake at 350 degrees for 20 minutes, or until set and edges are beginning to turn golden. Cool in pan on a wire rack. Cut into bars.

Chewy Gingerbread Bars

Marilyn Morel, Keene, NH

Hello Dolly Bars

My sister began making these in the late 1970s. Every time I need a little pick-me-up, I make these. My sister is no longer with us, but these wonderful treats hold some very special memories for me, which I've passed down to my children and now my grandson.

Makes one dozen

1/2 c. butter, softened
1 c. graham cracker crumbs
1 c. sweetened flaked coconut
6-oz. semi-sweet chocolate chips
6-oz. butterscotch chips
14-oz. can sweetened condensed
     milk
1 c. chopped pecans

Mix together butter and graham cracker crumbs; press into a lightly greased 9"x9" baking pan. Layer with coconut, chocolate chips and butterscotch chips. Pour condensed milk over top; sprinkle with pecans. Bake at 350 degrees for 25 to 30 minutes. Let cool; cut into bars.

Vickie, Gooseberry Patch

Blackberry Lemon Squares

Friends will be so impressed with these beautiful bar cookies...and they're really not hard to make!

Makes 2 dozen

2-1/4 c. all-purpose flour, divided
1/2 c. powdered sugar
1 c. cold butter, cut into pieces
4 eggs, beaten
2 c. sugar, divided
2 t. lemon zest
1/2 c. lemon juice
1 t. baking powder
1/4 t. salt
2 c. blackberries
Garnish: powdered sugar

Line the bottom and sides of a 13"x9" baking pan with aluminum foil, allowing 4 inches to extend over sides; lightly grease foil. Pulse 2 cups flour, powdered sugar and butter in a food processor 5 to 6 times, until mixture is crumbly. Press mixture into bottom of prepared pan. Bake at 350 degrees on low oven rack for 25 minutes, or just until golden. Whisk together eggs, 1-1/2 cups sugar, lemon zest and juice in a large bowl until blended. Combine baking powder, salt and remaining flour; whisk into egg mixture until blended. Pour mixture into prepared crust. Pulse blackberries and remaining sugar in a food processor 3 to 4 times, until blended. Transfer to a small saucepan. Cook over medium-low heat, stirring often, 5 minutes or until heated through. Pour through a fine wire-mesh strainer into a bowl, gently pressing blackberry mixture with back of a spoon; discard solids. Drizzle over mixture in pan. Bake at 350 degrees for 30 to 35 minutes, until filling is set. Let cool in pan on a wire rack 30 minutes. Lift from pan onto wire rack, using foil sides as handles; cool completely. Remove foil and cut into 2-inch squares; sprinkle with powdered sugar.

Blackberry Lemon Squares

Angie Stewart Forester, Memphis, TN

PB&J Breakfast Bars

This is our favorite quick breakfast item. My hubby can grab one of these as he walks out the door.

Makes one to 1-1/4 dozen

1-1/2 c. quick-cooking oats, uncooked
1/2 c. all-purpose flour
1/2 c. light brown sugar, packed
1/4 t. baking soda
1/4 t. salt
1/4 t. cinnamon
6 T. butter, melted
8-oz. pkg. cream cheese, softened
1/2 c. creamy peanut butter
1 egg, beaten
1/2 c. favorite-flavor jam

In a bowl, stir together oats, flour, brown sugar, baking soda, salt and cinnamon. Add melted butter and mix until crumbs form. Reserve 1/2 cup of oat mixture for topping; firmly spread remaining mixture in a lightly greased, parchment paper-lined 8"x8" baking pan. Bake at 350 degrees for 15 minutes, or until golden; cool. In a bowl, beat together cream cheese, peanut butter and egg. Spread cream cheese mixture over baked crust; spread with jam. Top with reserved oat mixture. Bake for an additional 30 minutes, or until topping is golden; cool. Refrigerate for one hour, or until fully set. Cut into bars.

Marilyn Rogers, Point Townsend, WA

Apricot Layer Bars

Stir in some chopped pecans for crunchiness.

Makes one to 1-1/2 dozen

1-3/4 c. quick-cooking oats, uncooked
1-3/4 c. all-purpose flour
1 c. brown sugar, packed
1 c. butter, softened
1/8 t. salt
12-oz. jar apricot preserves

Mix together oats, flour, brown sugar, butter and salt. Press half of mixture into a greased 11"x7" sheet pan. Spread preserves over the top and add remaining oat mixture. Bake at 350 degrees for 35 minutes. Let cool; cut into squares.

Apricot Layer Bars

Vickie, Gooseberry Patch

Raspberry Bars

Mix it up a bit by using another type of jam such as strawberry or blackberry.

Makes about 1-1/2 dozen

1 c. butter, softened
3/4 c. sugar
1 egg, beaten
1/2 t. vanilla extract
2-1/2 c. all-purpose flour
10-oz. jar seedless raspberry jam
1/2 c. chopped pecans, toasted

Beat butter and sugar in a large bowl until creamy. Add egg and vanilla, beating until blended. Add flour, beating until blended. Reserving one cup dough, press remaining dough firmly into a lightly greased 9"x9" baking pan. Spread jam evenly over crust. Stir pecans into reserved dough. Sprinkle evenly over jam layer. Bake at 350 degrees for 25 to 28 minutes, until golden. Cool completely in pan on a wire rack. Cut into bars.

Lynda McCormick, Burkburnett, TX

Quick & Easy Lemon Bars

An even simpler way to make a super-simple dessert. These tasty treats are perfect for whipping up to take to bake sales or potlucks.

Makes 2-1/2 dozen

16-oz. pkg. angel food cake mix
22-oz. can lemon pie filling
Optional: chopped pecans,
　　sweetened flaked coconut

Combine dry cake mix and pie filling in a large bowl; mix well. Spread in a greased 15"x10" jelly-roll pan; top with pecans or coconut, if desired. Bake at 350 degrees for 30 minutes. Let cool; cut into bars.

COOKIE KNOW-HOW
Many bar cookies freeze very well. Cut into bars and layer in a plastic container with a lid, separating layers with parchment or wax paper. Bar cookies will freeze well for up to 3 months.

Quick & Easy Lemon Bars

Gloria Suciu, Pensacola, FL

Coconut Crunch Pretzel Bars

I make these scrumptious salty-sweet bars every year for special occasions. They're my daughter's favorite dessert! You won't be able to eat just one.

Makes 3 dozen

15-1/4 oz. pkg. German chocolate
    cake mix
1/2 c. pretzels, crushed
1/2 c. butter, melted
3 eggs, divided
1/4 c. sugar
1 c. dark corn syrup
1 c. pecans, chopped
1 c. butterscotch chips
2-1/4 c. sweetened flaked coconut
1 c. semi-sweet chocolate chips

In a large bowl, combine dry cake mix, pretzels, butter and one egg. Beat with an electric mixer on low speed until well blended. Press mixture into a 13"x9" baking pan that has been lined with aluminum foil and sprayed with non-stick vegetable spray. Bake at 350 degrees for 15 minutes, or until crust puffs up and is dry. Cool 5 minutes. Meanwhile, combine sugar, corn syrup and remaining 2 eggs in a bowl. Beat with an electric mixer on low speed until well blended; fold in remaining ingredients. Spoon filling evenly over partially baked crust. Bake for 30 to 40 minutes longer, until edges are golden and center is almost set. Let cool one hour before slicing into bars.

Marie Stewart, Pensacola, FL

Apple-Cheddar Bars

If you love apples with cheese, these will be your new favorite bar.

Makes 2 to 3 dozen

1 c. brown sugar, packed
2 eggs, beaten
3 c. apples, peeled, cored and
    chopped
1 c. all-purpose flour
2 t. baking powder
1 t. salt
1 c. shredded Cheddar cheese
3/4 c. chopped nuts
1/4 c. sweetened flaked coconut

Combine brown sugar and eggs in a large bowl; stir well. Fold in apples. Combine flour, baking powder and salt in a separate bowl, stirring to mix. Add cheese, nuts and coconut to flour mixture, stirring to mix. Gradually add flour mixture to apple mixture, stirring just until combined. Spread batter in a greased and floured 13"x9" baking pan. Bake at 375 degrees for 20 to 25 minutes, until a toothpick inserted in center comes out clean. Let cool in pan on a wire rack for 10 minutes; cut into bars.

Apple-Cheddar Bars

Ardith Field, Goldfield, IA

Ann's Lemon Bars

These lemon bars were always the hit at family reunions. Ann was an amazing cook and everything was always done just right. These go so well with hot tea or a cup of coffee.

Makes 16 bars

1/2 c. butter, softened
6 T. powdered sugar
1 c. plus 2 T. all-purpose flour
2 eggs, beaten
2 T. lemon juice
1 T. lemon zest
1 c. sugar
1/2 t. baking powder
Garnish: powdered sugar

In a small bowl, mix together butter, powdered sugar and one cup flour. Press into a greased 8"x8" baking pan. Bake at 350 degrees for 12 minutes. Remove from oven and set aside. Combine eggs, lemon juice, lemon zest, sugar, remaining flour and baking powder. Pour into crust. Bake about 25 minutes until filling is set. Cool slightly. Sprinkle with powdered sugar.

Angela Hunker, Fostoria, OH

4-Layer Cookie Bars

A classic recipe...one bite and you'll know why!

Makes 2 dozen

16-oz. pkg. rectangular buttery
    crackers, divided
1/2 c. butter
2/3 c. sugar
1/2 c. brown sugar, packed
1 c. graham cracker crumbs
1/4 c. milk
2/3 c. creamy peanut butter
1/2 c. semi-sweet chocolate chips
1/2 c. peanut butter chips

Line the bottom of a buttered 13"x9" baking pan with a single layer of crackers; set aside. Melt butter in a heavy saucepan; add sugars, graham cracker crumbs and milk. Cook over medium-high heat until sugars dissolve, stirring often; spread over crackers in pan. Arrange another single layer of crackers on top; set aside. Combine remaining ingredients in a saucepan; cook over low heat until melted, stirring until smooth and creamy. Spread over crackers; set aside until firm. Cut into bars to serve.

4-Layer Cookie Bars

Tina Wright, Atlanta, GA

Pecan Pie Bars

Wonderful bars you can't stop eating! Great for a church social or potluck.

Makes 2 dozen

1-1/4 c. all-purpose flour
1/2 c. plus 3 T. brown sugar, packed and divided
1/2 c. plus 2 T. butter, divided
2 eggs
1/2 c. light corn syrup
1 t. vanilla
1/2 c. chopped pecans

Combine flour with 3 tablespoons brown sugar; cut in 1/2 cup butter until coarse crumbs form. Press mixture into a lightly greased 11"x7" baking pan. Bake at 375 degrees for 20 minutes. Meanwhile, beat eggs in a large bowl. Add remaining brown sugar, 2 tablespoons melted butter, corn syrup and vanilla; mix well. Fold in pecans; pour mixture into hot crust. Bake for 15 to 20 minutes. Cool and cut into bars.

Jodi Rhodes, Tolland, CT

Whole-Wheat Pumpkin Skillet Cake

This scrumptious recipe came out of the desire for a healthier cake. For a real show-stopper, top it with freshly whipped cream.

Makes 8 servings

1/4 c. butter, sliced
1/2 c. brown sugar, packed
1 egg, beaten
1/2 t. vanilla extract
1/2 ripe banana, mashed
1/3 c. canned pumpkin
1 c. whole-wheat flour
1/2 t. baking soda
1/4 t. salt
1/2 t. cinnamon
1/4 t. nutmeg
1/2 c. chopped walnuts
1/2 c. semi-sweet chocolate chips

Melt butter in a 9" cast-iron skillet over medium heat. Remove from heat; stir in brown sugar. Let cool. Whisk in egg; stir in vanilla. Add mashed banana and pumpkin; stir until blended and set aside. In a bowl, combine flour, baking soda, salt and spices. Add to pumpkin mixture in skillet; stir until well mixed. Stir in walnuts and chocolate chips; smooth top with spoon. Bake at 350 degrees for 15 to 20 minutes. Cut into wedges to serve.

Whole-Wheat Pumpkin Skillet Cake

Amy Prather, Longview, WA

Cream Cheese Bar Cookies

Coconut is a flavorful surprise in these creamy bar cookies!

Makes 3-1/2 to 4 dozen

2-1/4 c. all-purpose flour, divided
1 c. butter, softened
1/2 c. sugar
1/2 c. cornstarch
4 eggs, beaten
16-oz. pkg. brown sugar
1/2 t. baking powder
2 t. vanilla extract
1/2 c. chopped walnuts
1/2 c. sweetened flaked coconut

In a large bowl, combine 2 cups flour, butter, sugar and cornstarch with a pastry blender or 2 forks until mixture resembles fine crumbs. Press mixture evenly into an ungreased 15"x10" jelly-roll pan; bake at 350 degrees for 18 minutes. Beat eggs, brown sugar, remaining flour, baking powder and vanilla with an electric mixer on medium speed until blended; stir in walnuts and coconut. Spread on top of crust. Bake at 350 degrees for 30 minutes, or until set. Let cool in pan on a wire rack; spread with Cream Cheese Topping. Cut into bars.

Cream Cheese Topping:
8-oz. pkg. cream cheese, softened
1/2 c. butter, softened
1 t. vanilla extract
16-oz. pkg. powdered sugar

Beat first 3 ingredients with an electric mixer on medium speed until creamy; gradually add sugar, beating until blended.

Jean Burgon, Riverhead, NY

Apple Brownies

These apple bar cookies are just right for tucking into a lunchbox.

Makes one dozen

1/2 c. butter
1 c. sugar
1 egg, beaten
1 c. plus 1 T. all-purpose flour
1 t. cinnamon
1/2 t. baking soda
1/2 t. baking powder
1/4 t. salt
1 c. apple, peeled, cored and chopped
1 c. apple, cored and sliced

Mix all ingredients together except sliced apple. Press into an ungreased 17"x11" sheet pan. Arrange sliced apples on top. Bake at 350 degrees for 40 minutes. Cool; cut into bars.

Apple Brownies

Teresa Stiegelmeyer, Indianapolis, IN

Teresa's Tasty Apricot Bars

If you can't get to the beach, these apricot bars topped with coconut make you feel almost tropical.

Makes one dozen

1/2 c. butter, softened
1 c. all-purpose flour
1 t. baking powder
1 egg, beaten
1 T. milk
3/4 c. apricot preserves

Beat butter, flour and baking powder in a large bowl with an electric mixer at medium speed until blended. Stir in egg and milk. Press into a lightly greased 9"x9" baking pan; spread preserves over top and set aside. Prepare Coconut Topping and spread over preserves. Bake at 350 degrees for 25 to 30 minutes, until a toothpick inserted in center comes out clean. Cool completely in pan on a wire rack. Cut into bars.

Coconut Topping:
1/4 c. butter, softened
1 c. sugar
1 egg, beaten
1 t. vanilla extract
1 c. sweetened flaked coconut

Combine butter and sugar in a bowl, stirring until blended. Add egg and vanilla; stir well. Add coconut and stir until well blended.

Ruby Hempy, Largo, FL

Tropical Treat Bars

Cut into oversize bars...cookie lovers will be grateful!

Makes 2 dozen

1-1/2 c. graham cracker crumbs
1/2 c. butter, melted
14-oz. can sweetened condensed milk
1 c. white chocolate chips
1 c. sweetened dried pineapple, coarsely chopped
1-1/3 c. sweetened flaked coconut
1 c. macadamia nuts or almonds, coarsely chopped

Mix together graham cracker crumbs and melted butter. Press firmly into the bottom of an ungreased 13"x9" baking pan. Pour condensed milk evenly over crumb mixture. Sprinkle with chocolate chips, pineapple, coconut and nuts, pressing down firmly. Bake at 350 degrees for 25 to 30 minutes, until golden. Cool completely, chilling if desired. Cut into bars.

Tropical Treat Bars

Kris Axtell, Johnson City, TX

Banana Nut Bars

Everyone loves these bars. For a fancy dessert, serve with vanilla ice cream.

Makes one dozen

3 very ripe bananas, mashed
2 eggs, beaten
1/2 c. canola oil
1/2 c. plus 1 T. sugar, divided
1/2 c. quick-cooking oats, uncooked
1/2 c. whole-wheat flour
1/2 c. all-purpose flour
1/2 c. wheat germ
1 t. vanilla extract
1 t. baking powder
1/2 t. baking soda
1/4 t. salt
1/4 c. chopped walnuts

In a large bowl, stir together bananas, eggs, oil and 1/2 cup sugar until combined. Add remaining ingredients except walnuts and remaining sugar; stir just until blended. Pour batter into a greased 9"x9" baking pan. Sprinkle top with walnuts and remaining sugar. Bake at 350 degrees for 20 to 25 minutes, until golden and a toothpick tests clean. Cool and cut into squares.

June Sabatinos, Rigby, ID

Sour Cream Apple Squares

A good friend shared this recipe with me in the early 1980s. I have adapted it to suit my family's taste. We all love it!

Makes 1-1/2 dozen

2 c. all-purpose flour
2 c. brown sugar, packed
1/2 c. butter, softened
1 c. chopped walnuts or pecans
2 t. cinnamon
1 t. baking soda
1 t. salt
1 c. sour cream
1 egg, beaten
1 t. vanilla extract
2 c. Granny Smith apples, peeled, cored and finely chopped
Garnish: whipped cream or powdered sugar

Combine flour, brown sugar and butter in a large bowl. Beat with an electric mixer on low speed until fine crumbs form. Stir in nuts. Press 2-3/4 cups of crumb mixture firmly into an ungreased 13"x9" baking pan. To remaining crumb mixture, add cinnamon, baking soda, salt, sour cream, egg and vanilla. Stir well; fold in apples. Spoon apple mixture over crumb layer. Bake at 350 degrees for 30 to 40 minutes. Cool before cutting into squares. Top with whipped cream or a sprinkle of powdered sugar. Store loosely covered.

Sour Cream Apple Squares

Diane Axtell, Marble Falls, TX

Cran-Apple Crisscross Bars

Made with cranberries and apples and adorned with rich pie pastry, these colorful bars will steal the show. These bars freeze beautifully, so make them ahead of time and present them for a special treat.

Makes 3 dozen small bars

2 c. all-purpose flour
2 c. sugar, divided
1/2 t. vanilla extract
2 egg yolks, beaten
1 c. butter, softened
2 c. frozen cranberries
1 Granny Smith apple, cored and
    finely diced
2 T. frozen orange juice, thawed
2 T. cornstarch
1/8 t. ground ginger
1/2 t. salt
1/2 c. chopped nuts

For pastry, in a large bowl, mix flour, 1/2 cup sugar, vanilla and egg yolks. Cut in butter. Form into a ball and chill dough for one hour. In a food processor, pulse the frozen cranberries 5 or 6 times. In a saucepan, mix the cranberries and apple with the orange juice, remaining sugar, cornstarch, ginger and salt. Simmer over medium heat about 15 minutes, until thickened. Add chopped nuts. Chill. Press 2/3 of the pastry into an ungreased 13"x9" pan. Spread with cranberry-apple filling. Roll out remaining pastry to about 1/4-inch thickness. Cut pastry into 1/2-inch wide strips.

Arrange strips in a crisscross fashion over filling. Bake at 375 degrees for about 20 minutes. Cool and cut into squares or narrow rectangles.

Linda Nagy, Paris, KY

Double-Berry Nut Bars

If you like blueberries and cranberries, these will become your favorite bar. Any berry will work, so try blackberries if you prefer.

Makes 9 servings

2 eggs
1 c. sugar
1 c. all-purpose flour
1/3 c. butter, melted
1/2 c. blueberries, thawed if frozen
1/2 c. cranberries, thawed if frozen
1/2 c. chopped walnuts or pecans
Optional: powdered sugar

In a bowl, beat eggs with an electric mixer on medium speed until thick. Gradually beat in sugar until thoroughly blended. Stir in flour and melted butter; blend well. Add berries and nuts, mixing gently just until combined. Spread batter evenly in a greased 8"x8" baking pan. Bake at 350 degrees for 35 to 40 minutes, until golden. Cool; cut into squares. If desired, dust with powdered sugar.

Double-Berry Nut Bars

Polly McCallum, Palatka, FL

Mango Citrus Bars

Just a little change to the traditional lemon bar recipe...scrumptious!

Makes 1-1/2 dozen

1 c. butter, melted
1/2 c. powdered sugar
2-1/4 c. all-purpose flour, divided
4 eggs, beaten
2 c. sugar
1/4 c. mango juice
1 t. lemon or lime zest
Garnish: powdered sugar

In a small bowl, combine melted butter, powdered sugar and 2 cups flour. Press mixture into the bottom of a lightly greased 13"x9" baking pan. Bake at 350 degrees for 15 to 20 minutes; cool. Meanwhile, mix together remaining flour, eggs, sugar, juice and zest; pour over baked crust. Return to oven; bake an additional 20 minutes. Dust with powdered sugar. Cool and cut into bars.

Jeannine Mertz, Hurdsfield, ND

Corny Crunch Bars

If you like sweet & salty treats, you'll love these bars. Who would think to use savory corn chips with sugar and peanut butter? You will be surprised how yummy this combination is. It is like eating a piece of a salted nut roll candy bar!

Makes 2 dozen

2 c. light corn syrup
2 c. sugar
2 c. crunchy peanut butter
2 10-1/2 oz. pkgs. corn chips

In a large saucepan, combine corn syrup and sugar; bring to a boil over medium heat, stirring occasionally. Remove from heat; stir in peanut butter. Place corn chips in a large bowl coated with non-stick vegetable spray; stir in peanut butter mixture. Gently press into a buttered 18"x12" baking pan. Cool in pan on a wire rack until firm. Cut into small squares. Store in airtight container.

COOKIE KNOW-HOW
Dress up simple cookies with a yummy glaze. Combine 1/2 cup white chocolate chips with one teaspoon shortening in a microwave-safe bowl. Microwave on high for one minute; stir, then drizzle over cookies.

Corny Crunch Bars

Tracie Spencer, Rogers, KY

Scrumptious Pecan Turtle Bars

This recipe is one to turn to when you're asked to provide bake sale goodies...these delectable bites may be called "Turtles" but they'll go very quickly!

Makes 2 dozen

1/2 c. sugar
1/2 c. light corn syrup
3/4 c. creamy peanut butter
1 t. vanilla extract
3 c. corn flake cereal
1 c. chopped pecans
6-oz. pkg. semi-sweet chocolate chips
6-oz. pkg. butterscotch chips

In a saucepan over medium heat, bring sugar and corn syrup to a boil. Remove from heat. Stir in peanut butter, vanilla, cereal and pecans. Mix well and press into a greased 13"x9" baking pan. Melt chocolate chips and butterscotch chips in a small saucepan over low heat; stir until smooth. Spread chocolate mixture over bars. Cut into squares when cool.

Jennifer Martineau, Hillard, OH

Peanut Butter-Oat Bars

I put these bars on the dessert potluck table and everyone loves them!

Makes 2 dozen

1/2 c. whole-wheat flour
1 t. cinnamon
1/2 t. baking soda
1/8 t. sea salt
3/4 c. crunchy peanut butter
1/4 c. brown sugar, packed
1/3 c. honey
1 egg
2 egg whites
2 T. sunflower or olive oil
2 t. vanilla extract
2 c. long-cooking oats, uncooked
1 c. sweetened dried cranberries or raisins
1/2 c. sliced almonds
1/2 c. white or dark chocolate chips
Optional: chocolate frosting

Whisk together flour, cinnamon, baking soda and salt in a small bowl. In a separate bowl, beat peanut butter, brown sugar and honey with an electric mixer on medium speed. Beat egg and whites in a separate bowl; add to peanut butter mixture. Mix in oil and vanilla. Add flour mixture; stir in remaining ingredients. Spread into a greased 13"x9" baking pan, using the back of a spatula to spread easily. Bake at 350 degrees for 20 to 25 minutes. Cool; cut into squares.

Peanut Butter-Oat Bars

Lois Hobart, Stone Creek, OH

Lemon-Rosemary Zucchini Bars

These zucchini bars are the best! They smell wonderful while they bake and they taste so good.

Makes 2 dozen

3 c. all-purpose flour
1/2 t. baking powder
2 t. baking soda
2 T. fresh rosemary, minced
2 eggs
1-1/4 c. sugar
1/2 c. butter, melted and slightly cooled
1/4 c. olive oil
1 T. lemon zest
3 c. zucchini, grated

In a bowl, whisk together flour, baking powder, baking soda and rosemary; set aside. In a separate large bowl, beat eggs until frothy; beat in sugar, melted butter and olive oil. Stir in lemon zest and zucchini. Add flour mixture to egg mixture; stir until blended. Place batter in a 9"x9" pan sprayed with non-stick vegetable spray. Bake at 350 degrees for 20 to 30 minutes until a toothpick comes out clean. Cool completely before cutting into bars.

Kathleen Sturm, Corona, CA

Sweet Raspberry-Oat Bars

These layered bars with raspberry jam in the middle are my husband's favorite!

Makes 2-1/2 dozen

1/2 c. butter, softened
1 c. brown sugar, packed
1-1/2 c. all-purpose flour
1/2 t. baking soda
1/2 t. salt
1-1/2 c. long-cooking oats, uncooked
1/4 c. water
2/3 c. seedless raspberry jam
1 t. lemon juice

In a large bowl, blend together butter and brown sugar until fluffy; set aside. Combine flour, baking soda and salt in a separate bowl. Stir flour mixture into butter mixture. Add oats and water; mix together until crumbly. Firmly pat half of oat mixture into the bottom of a greased 13"x9" baking pan. In a small bowl, stir together jam and lemon juice; spread over oat mixture. Sprinkle remaining oat mixture over top. Bake at 350 degrees for 25 minutes. Cool completely before cutting into bars.

Sweet Raspberry-Oat Bars

Allison May, Seattle, WA

Lemon Chess Bars

These delicious bars freeze well...
keep some on hand to serve to
unexpected guests!

Makes 1-1/4 dozen

1/2 c. butter, softened
1 c. plus 2 T. all-purpose flour, sifted
    and divided
1/4 c. powdered sugar
2 eggs, beaten
1 c. sugar
zest of 1 lemon
3 T. lemon juice
Garnish: additional powdered sugar

In a bowl, beat butter with an electric
mixer at medium speed until fluffy.
Add one cup flour and 1/4 cup
powdered sugar and beat well; spoon
into an ungreased 8"x8" baking pan
and press firmly. Bake at 325 degrees
for 20 minutes. Meanwhile, combine
eggs, sugar, remaining flour, lemon
zest and lemon juice in a bowl. Mix
well; pour over baked bottom layer.
Bake 25 more minutes, or until
center is set. Cool. Sprinkle with
powdered sugar. Cut into bars.

Paula McFadden, Owensboro, KY

Nanny's Shortbread Chews

These bars are rich and chewy and
everyone asks for more!

Makes 2 dozen

1/2 c. butter, softened
1-1/2 c. brown sugar, packed and
    divided
1 c. plus 2 T. all-purpose flour,
    divided
2 eggs, beaten
1 t. baking powder
1 t. vanilla extract
1/2 t. salt
1-1/2 c. chopped dates or raisins
1 c. chopped walnuts or pecans

Mix together butter, 1/2 cup brown
sugar and one cup flour in a bowl
with a pastry blender or fork until
crumbly. Press butter mixture into
the bottom of a greased 13"x9" baking
pan. Bake at 350 degrees for 8 to
10 minutes; remove from oven. Mix
remaining brown sugar and flour,
eggs, baking powder, vanilla and salt;
blend well. Stir in dates or raisins
and nuts; pour mixture over baked
crust. Return to oven; bake 15 to
20 more minutes. Cool completely
and cut into squares.

Nanny's Shortbread Chews

Lillian Dahlstrom, Ames, IA

Maple-Walnut Bars

These are super yummy bars that our entire family loves...and they are gluten-free!

Makes 1-1/2 dozen

1 c. buckwheat flour
1 c. tapioca flour
1 t. baking soda
1/4 t. salt
1/2 c. rice bran
2 bananas, mashed
2/3 c. buttermilk
1/2 c. real maple syrup
1/4 c. oil
1 egg, beaten
2/3 c. walnuts

In a large bowl, mix buckwheat flour, tapioca flour, baking soda and salt. Add rice bran and mix well. Make a well in flour mixture. Set aside. In a medium bowl, mix bananas, buttermilk, maple syrup, oil and egg. Slowly pour banana mixture into flour mixture. Stir until just moistened. Fold in walnuts. Pour into an ungreased 9"x9" pan and bake at 350 degrees for about 20 minutes, until a toothpick inserted in the center comes out clean.

Valarie Lewis, Union Dale, PA

Oh, Harry! Bars

My mother handed down this dessert recipe to me. Growing up, it was a favorite among us kids!

Makes 2 dozen

3/4 c. butter, softened
1 c. dark brown sugar, packed
1/2 c. honey
1/2 t. ground ginger
4 c. quick-cooking oats, uncooked
6-oz. pkg. semi-sweet chocolate chips
2/3 c. creamy peanut butter

In a bowl, beat butter and brown sugar until light and fluffy. Beat in honey and ginger; stir in oats. With moistened hands, pat mixture into the bottom of a greased 13"x9" baking pan. Bake at 350 degrees until bubbly and lightly golden, about 25 minutes. In a microwave-safe bowl, heat chocolate chips and peanut butter on high for one minute. Stir; heat for another minute. Stir until all chips are melted. Spread chocolate mixture over bars and refrigerate until set. Cut into bars.

Oh, Harry! Bars

Noah Burnley, Ankeny, IA

Barbara's Scotcheroos

Barbara was an amazing cook and loved by everyone who knew her. We loved these bars every time she made them for us. They never lasted very long because we couldn't stop eating them!

Makes 16

1 c. corn syrup
1 c. sugar
1 c. creamy peanut butter
6 c. crispy rice cereal
1 c. semi-sweet chocolate chips
1 c. butterscotch chips

In a small saucepan, over medium heat, mix corn syrup and sugar. Boil for one minute; stir in peanut butter and cereal. Spread into a greased 13"x9" pan; let set until firm. In a double boiler, combine chocolate and butterscotch chips; cook until just melted. Spread on top of crispy rice mixture. Cool before cutting into squares.

Barbara Buckley, Edwards, MS

Luscious Banana Bars

Bananas and chocolate are a terrific combination. These bars are proof of that!

Makes 2-1/2 dozen

1/2 c. butter, softened
1 c. sugar
1 egg, beaten
1 t. vanilla extract
1-1/2 c. bananas, mashed
1-1/2 c. all-purpose flour
1 t. baking powder
1 t. baking soda
1/2 t. salt
1/4 c. baking cocoa

Beat together butter and sugar; add egg and vanilla. Blend until thoroughly combined; mix in bananas. Set aside. Combine flour, baking powder, baking soda and salt; blend into banana mixture. Divide batter in half; add cocoa to one half. Pour vanilla batter into a greased 13"x9" baking pan; spoon chocolate batter on top. Cut through batters with a knife to swirl. Bake at 350 degrees for 25 minutes. Cool and cut into bars.

Luscious Banana Bars

Jen Stout, Blandon, PA

Pineapple Goodie Bars

If you need a delicious quick & easy dessert, this is it!

Makes 2 dozen

18-oz. tube refrigerated sugar cookie
   dough
1 c. chopped pecans
1/2 c. candied pineapple, chopped
1/2 c. butterscotch chips
1/2 c. sweetened dried cranberries
1/2 c. sweetened flaked coconut

Place cookie dough in a bowl; stir until softened. Add remaining ingredients except coconut; mix well. Pat mixture evenly into a greased 13"x9" greased baking pan. Sprinkle coconut over top and press lightly. Bake at 325 degrees for 20 minutes. Cool; cut into bars.

COOKIE KNOW-HOW
Too cute! Top coconut bars with mini paper umbrellas...give to friends headed off to the beach or take to the next summertime picnic.

Donnie Carter, Wellington, TX

Quick & Easy Nutty Cheese Bars

This recipe is now the requested birthday gift of family & friends. They are so good cold!

Makes 2 dozen

18-1/2 oz. pkg. golden butter cake
   mix
1-1/2 c. chopped pecans or walnuts,
   divided
3/4 c. butter, melted
2 8-oz. pkgs. cream cheese, softened
1 c. brown sugar, packed

In a bowl, combine dry cake mix, 3/4 cup pecans and melted butter. Stir until well blended. Press mixture into the bottom of a greased 13"x9" baking pan. Combine cream cheese and brown sugar in a separate bowl. Stir until well mixed. Spread mixture evenly over crust. Sprinkle with remaining pecans. Bake at 350 degrees for 25 to 30 minutes, until edges are golden and cheese topping is set. Cool completely in pan on wire rack. Cut into bars. Refrigerate leftovers.

Quick & Easy Nutty Cheese Bars

Amy Tucker, British Columbia, Canada

Peanut Butter Bars

These will become your family's favorite bars. They are so moist and full of peanut-buttery flavor!

Makes 1-1/2 dozen

1 c. whole-wheat flour
1 c. long-cooking oats, uncooked
1-1/2 t. baking soda
1/4 c. creamy peanut butter
1/3 c. applesauce
1-1/2 c. milk
1/4 c. honey
2 T. finely chopped peanuts

Whisk together flour, oats and baking soda. Add peanut butter and applesauce; beat with an electric mixer on low speed until smooth. Stir in milk and honey. Spoon batter into ungreased 9"x9" pan. Sprinkle with chopped peanuts. Bake at 350 degrees for 20 to 25 minutes, until a toothpick tests clean. Cool; cut into squares.

Mary Ann Lewis, Olive Branch, MS

Best-Ever Granola Bar Cookies

These chewy, healthy bars are perfect to grab in the morning for a perfect take-along breakfast.

Makes one dozen

1 c. favorite granola
1 c. quick-cooking oats, uncooked
1/2 c. all-purpose flour
1/4 c. brown sugar, packed
1/8 t. cinnamon
1/2 c. unsalted mixed nuts, coarsely chopped
1/2 c. dried fruit, chopped into small pieces
2 T. ground flaxseed meal
1/4 c. canola oil
1/3 c. honey
1/2 t. vanilla extract
1 egg, beaten

Combine granola, oats and next 6 ingredients in a large bowl. Whisk together oil, honey and vanilla; stir into granola mixture. Add egg; stir to blend. Press mixture into a parchment paper-lined 8"x8" baking pan. Bake at 325 degrees for 30 to 35 minutes, until lightly golden around the edges. Remove from oven and cool 30 minutes to one hour. Slice into bars.

Best-Ever Granola Bar Cookies

Kendall Hale, Lynn, MA

Pumpkin Spice Bars

Perfect for any time you want a sweet and tender treat. Because you start with a cake mix, these bars are quick to make and stay moist for a long time.

Makes 2 dozen

18-1/4 oz. pkg. spice cake mix
1/2 c. plus 1 T. butter, melted and
 divided
1/2 c. pecans, finely chopped
1 T. plus 1 t. vanilla extract, divided
8-oz. pkg. cream cheese, softened
1/3 c. light brown sugar, packed
1 c. canned pumpkin
1 egg, beaten
1/2 c. white baking chocolate, finely
 chopped
1/3 c. long-cooking oats, uncooked
Optional: powdered sugar

Combine dry cake mix, 1/2 cup melted butter, pecans and one tablespoon vanilla, mixing well with a fork. Reserve one cup crumbs for streusel topping. Press remaining crumbs into a lightly greased 13"x9" baking pan. Bake at 350 degrees for 13 to 15 minutes, until puffy and set. Cool in pan on a wire rack 20 minutes. Meanwhile, beat cream cheese on medium speed with an electric mixer for 30 seconds, or until creamy. Add brown sugar, pumpkin, egg and remaining vanilla; beat until blended. Pour filling over baked crust. Stir white chocolate, remaining melted butter and oats into reserved streusel. Sprinkle over filling. Bake at 350 degrees for 30 minutes, or until edges begin to brown and center is set. Cool completely in pan on a wire rack. Sprinkle with powdered sugar, if desired. Cut into bars. Serve at room temperature or chilled.

Jan Stafford, Chickamauga, GA

Double Crunch Bars

My friend Debby shared this recipe with me. Her six children and my five children all love these scrumptious bars!

Makes 2 to 3 dozen

4 c. quick-cooking oats, uncooked
1 c. brown sugar, packed
3/4 c. butter, melted
1/2 c. honey
1/2 c. sweetened flaked coconut
1/2 c. semi-sweet chocolate chips
1/2 c. chopped nuts
1 t. vanilla extract
1 t. cinnamon
1 t. salt

Mix all ingredients together. Press mixture into a greased 15"x10" jelly-roll pan. Bake at 450 degrees for 10 to 12 minutes, until golden. Cool; cut into bars.

Double Crunch Bars

Favorite Holiday Sugar Cookies, p. 238

CHAPTER EIGHT

Holiday & Party Cookies

Be Mine Cherry Brownies, p. 247

Scaredy-Cat Cookies, p. 230

Mary Bettuchy, Saint Robert, MO

Apple Butter Thumbprints

These cookies remind me of fall in New England, where I grew up. I can almost feel the cool autumn breeze whenever I bake them.

Makes 2 dozen

1/2 c. butter, softened
3/4 c. brown sugar, packed
1 egg, beaten
1/2 t. vanilla extract
2 c. all-purpose flour
1/2 t. baking soda
1/2 t. cream of tartar
1/4 t. salt
1/2 c. sugar
1/2 c. apple butter

In a large bowl, stir together butter and brown sugar until well blended. Beat in egg; stir in vanilla and set aside. In a separate bowl, mix together flour, baking soda, cream of tartar and salt. Stir into butter mixture until well blended together. Place sugar in a small bowl; set aside. Scoop dough by rounded tablespoonfuls, shaping into balls. Roll balls in sugar, coating completely; place on parchment paper-lined baking sheets. Press your thumb into the center of each ball, creating an indentation. Spoon apple butter by teaspoonfuls into indentations; do not overfill. Bake at 350 degrees for 8 to 10 minutes, until just starting to set up but still soft. Cool on baking sheets for 5 minutes. Transfer cookies to wire racks and cool completely.

Jennifer Peterson, Ankeny, IA

Witches' Brooms

Any witch would love to have a sweet broom like these yummy cookies!

Makes about 4 dozen

1 c. butter, softened
2 c. brown sugar, packed
2 eggs, beaten
4-1/2 c. all-purpose flour
2 t. baking powder
1 t. baking soda
1/2 c. milk
1 t. vanilla extract
1 t. lemon extract
2 12-oz. pkgs. pretzel rods
Garnish: orange decorating sugar

In a large bowl, combine all ingredients except pretzels and garnish; mix well. Cover; refrigerate for one hour. Roll out dough 1/2-inch thick on a floured surface. Cut out triangle shapes. Place on greased and floured baking sheet with pretzel rod tucked underneath. Add strip of dough at top of triangle. Use a fork to score bottom of triangle. Sprinkle with orange sugar. Bake at 350 degrees for 10 minutes, or until golden around edges. Cool for one minute before removing from baking sheets; cool completely on wax paper.

Witches' Brooms

Claire Bertram, Lexington, KY

Tasty Cookie Pops

These cookies on a stick are always a fun treat at any party.

Makes 4-1/2 dozen

1 c. butter, softened
1 c. sugar
1 c. powdered sugar
2 eggs, beaten
3/4 c. oil
2 t. vanilla extract
4 c. all-purpose flour
1 t. baking soda
1 t. salt
1 t. cream of tartar
Garnish: candy sprinkles
54 lollipop sticks

Beat butter until fluffy; add sugars, beating well. Beat in eggs, oil and vanilla. In a separate bowl, combine flour and remaining ingredients except sprinkles. Add flour mixture to butter mixture and mix until well blended. Cover and chill 2 hours. Shape dough into 1-1/2 inch balls. Roll each ball in sprinkles, pressing gently, if needed, to coat. Place 2 inches apart on ungreased baking sheets. Insert a stick about one inch into each ball. Bake at 350 degrees for 10 to 11 minutes, until set. Let cool 2 minutes on baking sheets; cool completely on wire racks.

Athena Colegrove, Big Springs, TX

Spiderweb Cookies

Tuck these in cellophane bags, tie with twine and attach a spider ring... creepy and cute!

Makes 1-1/4 dozen

16-1/2 oz. tube refrigerated sugar
    cookie dough
3 c. powdered sugar
3 T. light corn syrup
1/2 t. vanilla extract
3 T. plus 3 t. milk, divided
2 T. baking cocoa

Slice dough into 16 rounds. Place 2 inches apart on ungreased baking sheets. Bake at 350 degrees for 12 to 14 minutes. Transfer to a wire rack to cool. Blend powdered sugar, corn syrup, vanilla and 3 tablespoons plus one teaspoon milk until smooth. Measure 1/3 cup of frosting mixture into a small bowl; stir in cocoa and remaining milk. Transfer chocolate frosting to a plastic zipping bag; snip off corner. Turn cookies so flat sides are up. Working on one cookie at a time, spread white frosting over top. Beginning in the center, pipe on a spiral of chocolate frosting. Starting in center of spiral, pull a knife tip through the spiral to create spiderweb pattern. Allow to set.

Spiderweb Cookies

Linda Doyle, West Seneca, NY

Peanut Butter Sandwich Dips

My grandchildren love these! They always enjoy them when they come to visit Grandma & Grandpa.

Makes 3 dozen

1/2 c. butter, softened
1-1/4 c. creamy peanut butter, divided
1 c. sugar
1 egg, beaten
1-1/2 c. all-purpose flour
3/4 t. baking soda
1/4 t. salt
1/4 c. powdered sugar
1 c. semi-sweet chocolate chips
4 t. oil

In a large bowl, beat butter, 1/2 cup peanut butter, sugar and egg until smooth. In a separate bowl, whisk together flour, baking soda and salt. Gradually beat flour mixture into butter mixture. Drop dough by rounded teaspoonfuls onto ungreased baking sheets. Bake at 350 degrees for 10 minutes, or until puffed. Cool for 2 minutes on baking sheets. Remove cookies to wire racks; let cool. Combine powdered sugar with remaining peanut butter; spread one rounded teaspoon on the flat side of half the cookies. Top with remaining cookies. Chill for 30 minutes. In a microwave-safe bowl, microwave chocolate chips and oil for one minute; stir until melted. Dip cookies halfway into melted chocolate. Let excess drip off. Refrigerate on wax paper-lined baking sheets until set.

Kay Marone, Des Moines, IA

Scaredy-Cat Cookies

Kids love to make and eat these cute Halloween goodies!

Makes 2 dozen

1 c. butter, softened
2 c. sugar
2 eggs, beaten
1 T. vanilla extract
3 c. all-purpose flour
1 c. baking cocoa
1/2 t. baking powder
1/2 t. baking soda
1/2 t. salt
48 pieces candy corn
24 red cinnamon candies

In a bowl, combine butter and sugar. Beat in eggs and vanilla; set aside. In a separate bowl, combine flour, cocoa, baking powder, baking soda and salt; gradually add to butter mixture. Form dough into 1-1/2 inch balls. Place on lightly greased baking sheets, 3 inches apart. Flatten balls with the bottom of a glass dipped in sugar. Pinch tops of cookies to form ears. For whiskers, press a fork twice into each cookie. Bake at 350 degrees for 7 to 8 minutes, until almost set. Remove from oven; immediately press on candy corn for eyes and cinnamon candies for noses. Remove to wire racks to cool.

Scaredy-Cat Cookies

Megan Brooks, Antioch, TN

Caramel-Filled Chocolate Cookies

I loved to help my Grandma Studer bake. She taught me how to make these wonderful cookies.

Makes 4 dozen

1 c. margarine, softened
1 c. brown sugar, packed
1 c. plus 1 T. sugar, divided
2 eggs, beaten
2 t. vanilla extract
2-1/4 c. all-purpose flour
3/4 c. baking cocoa
1 t. baking soda
1 c. chopped pecans, divided
48 chocolate-covered caramels,
    unwrapped

In a medium bowl, beat margarine, brown sugar and one cup sugar until fluffy. Stir in eggs and vanilla. In another bowl, combine flour, cocoa, baking soda and 1/2 cup pecans. Stir flour mixture into sugar mixture until combined. In a small bowl, mix remaining sugar with remaining pecans; set aside. For each cookie, shape one tablespoon dough around one caramel. Dip the dough ball, one side only, into pecan mixture. Place cookies, pecan-side up, on ungreased baking sheets. Bake at 375 degrees for 7 to 10 minutes. Cool on baking sheets 2 minutes; remove to a wire rack to cool completely.

Carissa Ellerd, Thomaston, ME

Winslow Whoopie Pies

This delicious and often-requested family recipe is a huge hit at any social gathering.

Makes one dozen

1/3 c. baking cocoa
1 c. sugar
1 egg, beaten
1/3 c. shortening, melted and cooled
3/4 c. milk
2 c. all-purpose flour
1 t. baking soda
1/8 t. salt
1 t. vanilla extract
Optional: chocolate sprinkles

In a bowl, combine cocoa and sugar. In another bowl, beat egg and shortening. Add egg mixture to cocoa mixture; stir in remaining ingredients except sprinkles. Drop dough by rounded tablespoonfuls onto lightly greased baking sheets. Bake at 350 degrees for 15 minutes. Let cool on wire racks. Spread the flat sides of half the cookies with Marshmallow Filling; top with remaining cookies. Roll edges in sprinkles, if using.

Marshmallow Filling:
2 c. powdered sugar
2/3 c. shortening
2 T. milk
1/3 c. plus 1 T. marshmallow creme
1 t. vanilla extract

Combine all ingredients in a large bowl; stir until smooth.

Winslow Whoopie Pies

Jamie Johnson, Columbus, OH

Rainbow Swirl Cookies

So pretty and playful...kids will love them!

Makes one dozen

3/4 c. butter, softened
3-oz. pkg. cream cheese, softened
1 c. sugar
1 egg, beaten
1 t. vanilla extract
2-3/4 c. all-purpose flour
1 t. baking powder
1/4 t. salt
purple, blue, yellow and pink gel
   paste colorings
12 lollipop sticks

In a bowl, beat butter, cream cheese and sugar until fluffy. Add egg and vanilla; beat until smooth and set aside. In a separate bowl, combine flour, baking powder and salt; mix well. Add flour mixture to butter mixture; stir until a soft dough forms. Divide dough evenly into 4 bowls. Tint each bowl with a different food coloring, mixing well to distribute color. Wrap dough separately in plastic wrap and chill for 2 hours. Roll dough into 3/4-inch balls. For each cookie, place one ball of each color together; roll to make one large ball and shape into a 12-inch-long rope. Starting at one end, coil rope to make a large round cookie. Place on lightly greased baking sheets, 3 inches apart. Insert lollipop sticks into cookies. Bake at 350 degrees for 8 to 10 minutes, until lightly golden. Cool on wire racks.

Jennifer Peterson, Ankeny, IA

Gingerbread Pinwheels

Gingerbread dough works perfectly for these clever pinwheel cookies.

Makes 20 cookies

1/2 c. brown sugar, packed
1/2 c. butter
2/3 c. molasses
2 eggs, beaten
3-1/2 c. all-purpose flour
1 T. baking powder
1 t. ground ginger
1 t. cinnamon
1/2 t. cloves
1/2 t. salt
Optional: frosting, gumdrops

Blend together brown sugar and butter until light and fluffy. Beat in molasses and eggs, beating well. In a separate bowl, sift together flour, baking powder, spices and salt. Add flour mixture to sugar mixture; mix well. Cover and refrigerate for 2 hours. Divide dough into fourths. On a floured surface, roll dough out to 1/4-inch thickness. Cut into 3" squares. Place on greased baking sheets. Cut in from corners and fold each to center to form a pinwheel. Bake at 350 degrees for 5 to 7 minutes, until dark golden. Cool slightly on pans before removing to wire racks to cool completely. Pipe with Frosting and add gumdrop to center if desired.

Frosting:
3 c. powdered sugar
3 T. butter, melted
3 T. milk
1 t. vanilla extract

Combine all ingredients in a medium bowl. Beat with an electric mixer on low speed until smooth.

Gingerbread Pinwheels

Sandy Bootham, Camden, MI

Graham Pralines

A friend gave me this easy recipe...
it's wonderful for the holidays. Yes, it
calls for both butter and margarine
for twice the flavor!

Makes about 2 dozen

1 sleeve graham crackers
1/2 c. butter, sliced
1/2 c. margarine, sliced
1 c. brown sugar, packed
1/8 t. salt
1 c. chopped pecans

Cover a baking sheet with aluminum
foil; spray lightly with non-stick
vegetable spray. Break crackers and
arrange on baking sheet; set aside.
Combine butter, margarine, sugar
and salt in a saucepan over low heat,
stirring well. Bring to a boil and
boil for 2 minutes; pour evenly over
crackers. Sprinkle with pecans; bake
at 350 degrees for 10 to 12 minutes.
Let cool; break apart. Store in a
covered container.

Carol Field Dahlstrom, Ankeny, IA

Fruitcake Bars

This recipe came from my
grandmother and was originally a
loaf fruitcake. But we like it made into
these heavenly bars.

Makes 2-1/2 dozen

1 c. butter, softened
1 c. sugar
5 eggs
1/2 c. orange juice
1 c. grape jelly
2-1/2 c. all-purpose flour
1 t. baking powder
1/2 t. salt
1 t. cinnamon
1/2 t. each ground nutmeg, ground
    allspice, ground cloves
3/4 c. candied cherries
1/2 c. slivered almonds
3/4 c. chopped pecans
1/2 c. golden raisins
1/2 c. raisins
1/2 c. dried apricots, chopped
1/2 c. candied orange peel, chopped
3/4 c. chopped dates
3/4 c. shredded coconut

Line the bottom of 2 greased
8"x8" pans with wax paper. In a large
bowl, cream butter and sugar. Add
eggs one at a time and beat well. Add
orange juice and jelly and mix well.
In a separate bowl, mix flour, baking
powder, salt and spices. Add to butter
mixture. In a large bowl, mix all fruits
and nuts. Fold into flour mixture.
Pour into prepared pans and bake
at 325 degrees for about 35 minutes,
until golden. Cut into bars.

Fruitcake Bars

Jen Licon-Connor, Gooseberry Patch

Minty Candy Canes

Easy spritz dough is dressed up for the holidays with a dip of white chocolate and a sprinkle of peppermint.

Makes 5 dozen

3/4 c. butter, softened
1/2 c. sugar
1 t. baking powder
1 egg, beaten
1/2 t. peppermint extract
1-3/4 c. all-purpose flour
6 1-oz. sqs. white baking chocolate
1 T. shortening
1/3 c. peppermint candies, finely
    crushed

In a large bowl, combine butter, sugar and baking powder. Beat with an electric mixer on medium speed until mixed. Add egg and extract; blend well. Beat in as much flour as possible with mixer; stir in any remaining flour. Pack dough into a cookie press fitted with a 1/2-inch star plate. Press out dough to form 4-inch sticks on ungreased baking sheets, one inch apart; bend into a candy cane shape. Bake at 375 degrees for 7 to 9 minutes, until edges are firm but not brown. Let cool on a wire rack. Melt white chocolate with shortening in a small heavy saucepan over low heat, stirring frequently. Dip the end of each cane into chocolate, letting any excess drip off. Place on wax paper; sprinkle with crushed candies. Let stand until set.

Diana Hamilton, Beaverton, OR

Favorite Holiday Sugar Cookies

These are the best sugar cookies ever! Use your favorite cutters and decorate with the ones you love.

Makes 3 dozen

3/4 c. butter
1 c. sugar
2 eggs, beaten
1 t. almond extract
3 c. all-purpose flour
1/2 t. baking powder
1 t. baking soda
1/2 t. salt
Garnish: candy sprinkles

Beat together butter and sugar until creamy. Add eggs and almond extract and beat well. Mix together flour, baking powder, baking soda and salt in a bowl. Add to butter mixture and beat well. Wrap dough in plastic wrap; refrigerate for 30 minutes. On a floured surface, roll out dough 1/8-inch thick; cut out with cookie cutters. Arrange on lightly greased baking sheets. Bake at 375 degrees for 5 to 6 minutes, until lightly golden. Cool. Frost using one tablespoon of Sugar Cookie Frosting per cookie. Decorate as desired.

Sugar Cookie Frosting:
4 c. powdered sugar
2 T. butter, melted
3 T. milk

Mix all ingredients together until smooth.

Favorite Holiday Sugar Cookies

Tina Knotts, Cable, OH

Best Sugar Cookies

Everyone needs a dependable cut-out cookie recipe for Christmas...this is mine!

Makes 4 dozen

2 c. butter, softened
1-1/3 c. sugar
2 eggs, beaten
2 t. vanilla extract
5 c. all-purpose flour

In a large bowl, blend butter and sugar together; stir in eggs and vanilla. Add flour; mix until well blended. Shape dough into a ball; cover and chill for 4 hours to overnight. Roll out dough 1/4-inch thick on a lightly floured surface. Cut out with cookie cutters as desired. Arrange cookies on lightly greased baking sheets. Bake at 350 degrees for 8 to 10 minutes, until golden. Cool on wire racks. Frost cookies when cool. For Sugar Cookie Frosting recipe, see page 238.

JoAnn, Gooseberry Patch

Big Crunchy Sugar Cookies

These goodies earned their name from a coating of coarse sugar.

Makes 1-1/2 dozen

1 c. butter, softened
1 c. sugar
1 egg
1-1/2 t. vanilla extract
2 c. all-purpose flour
1/2 t. baking powder
1/4 t. salt
Garnish: assorted coarse decorator sugars

Beat butter with an electric mixer on medium speed until creamy. Gradually add sugar, beating until smooth. Add egg and vanilla, beating until blended. Combine flour, baking powder and salt; gradually add to butter mixture, beating just until blended. Shape dough into a ball; cover and chill 2 hours. Divide dough into 3 portions. Work with one portion at a time, storing remaining dough in refrigerator. Shape dough into 1-1/2 inch balls; roll each ball in decorator sugar. Place 2 inches apart on parchment paper-lined baking sheets. Gently press and flatten each ball of dough to 3/4-inch thickness. Bake at 375 degrees for 13 to 15 minutes, until edges of cookies are lightly golden. Cool 5 minutes on baking sheets; remove to wire racks to cool.

Big Crunchy Sugar Cookies

Peggy Cummings, Cibolo, TX

Peppermint Meringues

Use the ice pulse button on your blender to make quick work of crushing the candies.

Makes 3 dozen

2 egg whites
1/8 t. cream of tartar
1/8 t. salt
3/4 c. sugar
2 c. mini semi-sweet chocolate chips
3 T. crushed peppermint candies
1/2 t. vanilla extract

Beat egg whites in a large bowl with an electric mixer at high speed until foamy. Add cream of tartar and salt, beating until mixed; gradually add sugar, one tablespoon at a time, beating well after each addition until stiff peaks form. Gently fold in remaining ingredients. Drop by teaspoonfuls 1-1/2 inches apart onto greased baking sheets. Bake at 250 degrees for 40 minutes, or until dry. Remove to wire racks to cool completely. Store in an air-tight container

Jennifer Martineau, Delaware, OH

Candy Cane Thumbprints

My little daughter insists on making the thumbprints herself...won't Santa love finding a plate of these cookies on Christmas Eve!

Makes about 3 dozen

2/3 c. butter, softened
1/2 c. sugar
1/4 t. salt
1 egg, beaten
1 t. vanilla extract
1-1/2 c. all-purpose flour
Garnish: finely crushed peppermint
    candies

With an electric mixer on low speed, blend butter, sugar and salt. Mix in egg and vanilla. Beat in as much flour as possible; stir in remaining flour. Cover; chill for one hour. Shape dough into one-inch balls; place 2 inches apart on ungreased baking sheets. Bake at 375 degrees for 8 to 10 minutes, until lightly golden around edges. Remove from oven; make a thumbprint in each cookie with thumb. Cool. Pipe Filling into centers; sprinkle with crushed candies.

Filling:
1/4 c. butter, softened
1/4 t. peppermint extract
1-1/2 c. powdered sugar
2 to 3 t. milk

Blend butter and extract. Gradually add powdered sugar and milk to a piping consistency.

Candy Cane Thumbprints

Darlene Hollingsworth, Urbandale, IA

Gingerbread Cut-Out Cookies

There are so many Christmas gingerbread cookies that folks like to make...this is our favorite.

Makes 2 dozen

1/4 c. shortening
1/4 c. butter, softened
1/2 c. sugar
1 t. ground ginger
1/2 t. cinnamon
1/2 t. ground cloves
1/4 t. nutmeg
1/4 t. salt
1 egg, beaten
1/2 c. molasses
1 T. cider vinegar
1/2 t. baking soda
1 t. baking powder
3 c. all-purpose flour
Optional: decorative candies

In a large bowl, beat shortening and butter with an electric mixer on medium to high speed until creamy. Add the sugar, spices, salt, egg and molasses. Beat in vinegar, baking soda, baking powder and flour. Divide dough in half. Cover and chill about one hour or until dough is easy to handle. On a lightly floured surface, roll out one portion and cut out shapes, rerolling scraps as needed. Place cut-outs one inch apart on ungreased baking sheets. Bake at 375 degrees for 6 to 8 minutes, until edges are lightly browned. Cool on cookie sheet for one minute. Transfer to a wire rack and let cool. If desired, decorate cookies with Powdered Sugar Icing.

Powdered Sugar Icing:
2 c. powdered sugar, sifted
1 T. butter, melted
2 T. milk
1 t. vanilla extract
Optional: few drops food coloring

Combine all ingredients in a large bowl. Beat with an electric mixer on low speed until smooth.

COOKIE KNOW-HOW
No time to decorate now? Bake and store cookies until ready to decorate. Place cooled cookies in layers separated by wax paper in an airtight container. Freeze until ready to use up to 3 months.

Gingerbread Cut-Out Cookies

Anna McMaster, Portland, OR

Easter Ice Cream Sandwiches

Wrap these springtime treats in pastel-colored plastic wrap and store in the freezer until ready to serve.

Makes about one dozen

2 c. butter, softened
1-1/3 c. sugar
2 eggs, beaten
2 t. vanilla extract
5 c. all-purpose flour
assorted food colorings
1 pt. vanilla ice cream, softened
Optional: 2 c. sweetened flaked
    coconut

Blend butter and sugar together; stir in eggs and vanilla. Add flour; mix until well blended. Shape into a ball; cover and chill for 4 hours to overnight. Reserve one tablespoon of dough for each color. Roll out remaining dough on a floured surface 1/4-inch thick. Use a 3-inch egg-shaped cookie cutter to cut dough. Tint reserved dough with food coloring as desired. Form colored dough into small balls and ropes and arrange on half the cookies. Place on ungreased baking sheets. Bake at 350 degrees for 7 to 9 minutes. Cool on baking sheets one minute; remove cookies to cool completely on wire rack. Position plain cookie on bottom, spread with ice cream and top with decorated cookie. Gently press together; freeze until serving time. If desired, mix a few drops of green food coloring and coconut; let dry on wax paper. Place cookies on colored coconut.

Dana Cunningham, Lafayette, LA

Be Mine Cherry Brownies

Bake an extra-sweet Valentine for your sweetie!

Makes 14

18.3-oz. pkg. fudge brownie mix
3 1-oz. sqs. white baking chocolate
1/3 c. whipping cream
1 c. cream cheese frosting
1/4 c. maraschino cherries, drained
** and chopped**
1-1/2 c. semi-sweet chocolate chips
1/4 c. butter
Garnish: candy sprinkles

Prepare brownie mix according to package instructions; set aside batter. Line a 13"x9" baking pan with aluminum foil, leaving several inches on 2 sides for handles. Spray bottom of foil with non-stick vegetable spray; spread batter into pan. Bake at 350 degrees for 24 to 26 minutes; let cool. Lift brownies from pan; remove foil. Use a 3-inch heart-shaped cookie cutter to cut brownies. In a microwave-safe bowl, melt white baking chocolate and whipping cream for one to 2 minutes, stirring until chocolate is melted; refrigerate 30 minutes. Stir frosting and cherries into chilled chocolate mixture; spread over brownies. In a microwave-safe bowl, melt chocolate chips and butter for one to 2 minutes, stirring until smooth. Transfer to a plastic zipping bag, snip off one corner tip and drizzle over brownies. Garnish with sprinkles.

Index

BAR COOKIES

4-Layer Cookie Bars, p194

Ann's Lemon Bars, p194

Apple-Cheddar Bars, p192

Applesauce Spice Bars, p180

Apricot Layer Bars, p188

Banana Nut Bars, p202

Barbara's Scotcheroos, p216

Best-Ever Granola Bar Cookies, p220

Blackberry Lemon Squares, p186

Chewy Gingerbread Bars, p184

Choco-Berry Goodie Bars, p178

Coconut Crunch Pretzel Bars, p192

Corny Crunch Bars, p206

Cran-Apple Crisscross Bars, p204

Cranberry Crumb Bars, p182

Cream Cheese Bar Cookies, p198

Dorothy's Raisin Bars, p184

Double-Berry Nut Bars, p204

Double Crunch Bars, p222

Gail's Pumpkin Bars, p178

Gooey Toffee Scotchies, p180

Grandma Gray's Spice-Nut Bars, p174

Hello Dolly Bars, p186

Lemon Chess Bars, p212

Lemon-Rosemary Zucchini Bars, p210

Luscious Banana Bars, p216

Mango Citrus Bars, p206

Maple-Walnut Bars, p214

Nanny's Shortbread Chews, p212

Oh, Harry! Bars, p214

PB&J Breakfast Bars, p188

Peach Mango Melba Shortbread Bars, p176

Peanut Butter Bars, p220

Peanut Butter-Oat Bars, p208

Pecan Pie Bars, p196

Pineapple Goodie Bars, p218

Pumpkin Spice Bars, p222

Quick & Easy Lemon Bars, p190

Quick & Easy Nutty Cheese Bars, p218

Raspberry Bars, p190

Salted Nut Squares, p182

Scrumptious Pecan Turtle Bars, p208

Snowy Glazed Apple Squares, p174

Sour Cream Apple Squares, p202

Staycation Coconut-Lime Bars, p176

Sweet Raspberry-Oat Bars, p210

Teresa's Tasty Apricot Bars, p200

Tropical Treat Bars, p200

Whole-Wheat Pumpkin Skillet Cake, p196

BROWNIES & BLONDIES

Apple Brownies, p198

Birthday Brownies, p68

Brownie Buttons, p62

Brown Sugar Brownies, p66

Buckeye Brownies, p60

Cake Mix Brownies, p76

Chocolate-Butter Cream
   Squares, p70

Chocolate Cappuccino Brownies,
   p82

Chocolate Coconut Brownies,
   p84

Chocolate Hazelnut Skillet Bars,
   p60

Coconut-Pecan Fudge Brownies,
   p64

Cookies & Cream Brownies, p68

Divine Praline Brownies, p80

Double Chocolate-Mint
   Brownies, p64

Double-Dark Chocolate
   Brownies, p66

Easy 4-Layer Marshmallow
   Brownies, p72

Fabulous Zucchini Brownies, p58

Fudge Brownie Pie, p80

German Chocolate Cookie. Bars,
   p72

Mother's Zucchini Brownies, p82

Peanut Butter Brownies, p58

Quarterback Crunch Brownies,
   p74

Red Velvet Brownies, p76

Rocky Road Bars, p62

Speedy Little Devils, p70

Swirled Peanut Butter
   Cheesecake Bars, p84

The Best Blondies, p74

Tiger's Eye Brownies, p78

Triple-Layered Brownies, p78

CUT-OUT COOKIES

Best Sugar Cookies, p162

Buttermilk Sugar Cookies, p160

Butterscotch Gingerbread
   Cookies, p166

Dipped Gingerbread Stars, p160

Easiest-Ever Sugar Cookies, p170

Emily's Gingerbread Cookies, p164

Gingerbread Babies, p168

Gingerbread Cookies, p158

Good Neighbor Sugar Cookies, p156

Homemade Graham Crackers, p168

Quick Sugar Cookies, p162

Raisin-Filled Cookies, p170

Spirited Raisin Cookies, p158

Swig Cookies, p166

DROP COOKIES

Blueberry Drop Cookies, p118

Breakfast Cookies, p138

Brown Sugar-Apple Cookies, p126

Carol's Famous Chocolate Chip Cookies, p148

Cherry Macaroons, p130

Chocolate Chip-Oat Cookies, p126

Chocolate Chip Tea Cookies, p150

Coconut-Lime Macaroons, p136

Cool Mint Chocolate Swirls, p114

Double Chocolate Cookies, p122

Espresso Bean Cookies, p150

Favorite Chocolate Chippers, p132

"Free" Coconut Cookies, p142

Frosted Cherry Drops, p152

German Chocolate Delights, p130

Grab & Go Breakfast Cookies, p146

Gram's Zucchini Cookies, p120

Grandma Mitten's Oatmeal Cookies, p128

Grandma's Pecan Balls, p132

Granny's Chocolate Fudge Cookies, p142

Healthy Morning Cookies, p144

Iced Carrot Cookies, p134

Lacy Florentine Cookies, p116

Lemon-Macadamia Cookies, p148

Madelene's Buttermilk-Molasses Cookies, p140

Mincemeat Cookies, p120

Mix-and-Go Chocolate Cookies, p116

Mom's Monster Cookies, p118

Nellie's Persimmon Cookies, p138

Oatmeal-Carrot Cookies, p146

Oatmeal-Raisin Spice Cookies, p136

Orange Cranberry Cookies, p140

Pineapple Nut Cookies, p122

Simple Meringues, p124

Snowcap Cookies, p128

Soft Pumpkin Cookies, p114

Speedy Peanut Butter Cookies, p134

The Best Oatmeal Cookies, p152

White Chocolate Cookies, p124

White Chocolate Macaroons, p144

FANCY & SPECIALTY COOKIES

Almond Cream Spritz, p102

Baklava Cookies, p88

Chocolate Waffle Sticks, p100

Crunchy Biscotti, p110

Dad's Giant Cookie, p96

French Macaroons, p98

German Apple Streusel Kuchen, p90

Grandmother's Waffle Cookies, p90

Italian Cheese Cookies, p106

Mexican Tea Cookies, p108

Mom's Italian Cookies, p100

Norwegian Kringla, p104

Raspberry Almond Bars, p108

Raspberry Linzer Tarts, p88

Raspberry-Marshmallow Cookie Pizza, p110

Russian Tea Cookies, p96

Sour Cream Drop Cookies, p106

Stained Glass Cookies, p92

Swedish Ginger Cookies, p102

FROSTINGS & FILLINGS

Browned Butter Frosting, p180

Butter Frosting, p20

Cherry Frosting, p152

Citrus Icing, p134

Coconut Topping, p200

Cream Cheese Frosting, p76, 178

Cream Cheese Topping, p198

Crumb Topping, p32

Filling, p70, 242

Frosting, p164, 235

Glaze, p114

Icing, p70

Marshmallow Filling, p232

Peanut Butter Frosting, p58

Peppermint Filling, p242

Powdered Sugar Icing, p104, 156, 162, 244

Raisin Filling, p170

Royal Icing, p94

Simple Frosting, p42

Simple Powdered Sugar Frosting, p166

Sugar Cookie Frosting, p238

Sweet Vanilla Icing, p106

Toffee Sauce, p180

Vanilla Filling, p28, 98

Whipped Cream Filling, p70

HOLIDAY & PARTY COOKIES

Apple Butter Thumbprints, p226

Be Mine Cherry Brownies, p247

Best Sugar Cookies, p240

Big Crunchy Sugar Cookies, p240

Candy Cane Thumbprints, p242

Caramel-Filled Chocolate Cookies, p232

Easter Ice Cream Sandwiches, p246

Favorite Holiday Sugar Cookies, p238

Fruitcake Bars, p236

Gingerbread Cut-Out Cookies, p244

Gingerbread Pinwheels, p234

Graham Pralines, p236

Minty Candy Canes, p238

Peanut Butter Sandwich Dips, p230

Peppermint Meringues, p242

Rainbow Swirl Cookies, p234

Scaredy-Cat Cookies, p230

Spiderweb Cookies, p228

Tasty Cookie Pops, p228

Winslow Whoopie Pies, p232

Witches' Brooms, p226

ICEBOX/REFRIGERATOR COOKIES

Almond Butter Slices, p40

Dazzling Neapolitan Cookies, p44

Grandma Saint's Fridge Cookies, p46

Hazelnut Pinwheels, p44

Hopscotch Cookies, p52

Key Lime Bites, p42

Lemon Slice Cookies, p36
Mint-Chocolate Sandwiches, p54
Peanut Butter-Chocolate Bars,
    p48
Pretty Swirl Cookies, p50
Spicy Maple-Anise Snaps, p36

NO-BAKE COOKIES
Cale's Corn Flake Cookies, p40
Chocolate Almond Oatmeal
    Cookies, p36
Chocolate-Orange Snowballs,
    p42
Favorite Cocoa No Bake, p52
Graham No-Bake Cookies, p54
No-Bake Granola Bars, p46
No-Bake Peanut Butter Bars, p50
No-Bake Yummy Balls, p48
Snowballs, p38

ROLLED & SHAPED COOKIES
Apple Crisp Cookies, p32
Butterscotch Cookies, p32
Buttery Ricotta Cookies, p12
Cherry-Cardamom Cookies, p16
Cinnamon Gingersnaps, p22
Cinnamon-Sugar Butter Cookies,
    p26
Cranberry-Sugar Sandies, p30
Favorite Sugar Cookies, p28
Fudgy Cappuccino Crinkles, p24
Grandma Miller's Nutmeg Logs,
    p20

Grandma's Pecan Balls, p26
Ice Cream Nut Roll Crescents,
    p10
Lemon Snowdrops, p24
Molasses Sugar Cookies, p12
Mom & Me Peanut Butter Kisses,
    p10
Nanny's Peanut Butter Goblins,
    p30
Peanut Butter Surprise Cookies,
    p14
Pecan Cookie Balls, p14
Pistachio Thumbprints, p28
Raspberry-Almond Shortbread
    Cookies, p18
Snickerdoodles, p22
Sugar-Topped Cookies, p18
Twist Cookies, p16
White Chocolate-Cranberry
    Cookies, p20

U.S. to Metric Recipe Equivalents

Volume Measurements

1/4 teaspoon. . . . . 1 mL
1/2 teaspoon . . . . .2 mL
1 teaspoon . . . . .5 mL
1 tablespoon = 3 teaspoons . . . 15 mL
2 tablespoons = 1 fluid ounce . 30 mL
1/4 cup. 60 mL
1/3 cup. .75 mL
1/2 cup = 4 fluid ounces. . . . . .125 mL
1 cup = 8 fluid ounces . . . . . . 250 mL
2 cups=1 pint=16 fluid ounces 500 mL
4 cups =1 quart . . . . .75 mL

Weights

1 ounce .30 g
4 ounces . . . . 120 g
8 ounces . . . . .225 g
16 ounces = 1 pound . . . . 450 g

Baking Pan Sizes
Square
8x8x2 inches . . . . 2 L = 20x20x5 cm
9x9x2 inches . . . 2.5 L = 23x23x5 cm

Rectangular
13x9x2 inches. . . 3.5 L = 33x23x5 cm
Loaf
9x5x3 inches . . . . . 2 L = 23x13x7 cm

Round
8x1½ inches . . . . .1.2 L = 20x4 cm
9x1½ inches . . . . .1.5 L = 23x4 cm

Recipe Abbreviations

t. = teaspoon   ltr. = liter
T. = tablespoon   oz. = ounce
c. = cup   lb. = pound
pt. = pint   doz. = dozen
qt. = quart   pkg. = package
gal. = gallon   env. = envelope

Oven Temperatures

300° F .150° C
325° F .160° C
350° F .180° C
375° F .190° C
400° F . . . . 200° C
450° F .230° C

Kitchen Measurements

A pinch = 1/8 tablespoon
1 fluid ounce = 2 tablespoons
3 teaspoons = 1 tablespoon
4 fluid ounces = 1/2 cup
2 tablespoons = 1/8 cup
8 fluid ounces = 1 cup
4 tablespoons = 1/4 cup
16 fluid ounces = 1 pint
8 tablespoons = 1/2 cup
32 fluid ounces = 1 quart
16 tablespoons = 1 cup
16 ounces net weight = 1 pound
2 cups = 1 pint
4 cups = 1 quart
4 quarts = 1 gallon

Send us your favorite recipe

and the memory that makes it special for you!*

If we select your recipe for a brand-new **Gooseberry Patch** cookbook, your name will appear right along with it...and you'll receive a FREE copy of the book!

Submit your recipe on our website at

www.gooseberrypatch.com/sharearecipe

*Please include the number of servings and all other necessary information.

Have a taste for more?

Visit www.gooseberrypatch.com to join our Circle of Friends!

• Free recipes, tips and ideas plus a complete cookbook Index
• Get mouthwatering recipes and special email offers delivered to your inbox.

You'll also love these cookbooks from **Gooseberry Patch**!

A Year of Holidays
Christmas for Sharing
Classic Church Potlucks
Fresh & Easy Family Meals
Mom's Best Sunday Dinners
Our Best 5-Ingredient Fresh Family Recipes
Our Best Blue Ribbon Recipes
Our Best Fast, Easy & Delicious Recipes
Our Best Recipes for Cast Iron Cooking
Quick & Easy Recipes with Help from My Instant Pot,
Air Fryer, Slow Cooker, Waffle Iron & more

www.gooseberrypatch.com

From our Kitchen to Yours

Our Story

Back in 1984, our families were neighbors in little Delaware, Ohio. With small children, we wanted to do what we loved and stay home with the kids too. We had always shared a love of home cooking and so, **Gooseberry Patch** was born.

Almost immediately, we found a connection with our customers and it wasn't long before these friends started sharing recipes. Since then we've enjoyed publishing hundreds of cookbooks with your tried & true recipes.

We know we couldn't have done it without our

friends all across the country and we look forward to continuing to build a community with you. Welcome to the **Gooseberry Patch** family!

Jo Ann & Vickie